INTERMEDIATE

SHARE the Music

MACMILLAN McGRAW-HILL

MÚSICA PARA TODOS

SONGS, GAMES, AND TEACHER RESOURCES

Macmillan/McGraw-Hill School Publishing Company

New York • Columbus

PROJECT AUTHOR

Mollie Tower

WRITERS AND CONSULTANTS

Deborah Acevedo

Maria Yolanda Garza

Kay Greenhaw

Pablo Ortiz

Ana Peluffo

Barb Stevanson

Rose Zuñiga

SERIES AUTHORS

Judy Bond, *Coordinating Author*

René Boyer-White

Margaret Campbelle-duGard

Marilyn Copeland Davidson, *Coordinating Author*

Robert de Frece

Mary Goetze, *Coordinating Author*

Doug Goodkin

Betsy M. Henderson

Michael Jothen

Carol King

Vincent P. Lawrence, *Coordinating Author*

Nancy L. T. Miller

Ivy Rawlins

Susan Snyder, *Coordinating Author*

COVER ILLUSTRATION   David Diaz

ILLUSTRATION CREDITS   Anthony Accardo, 74, 92; Fian Arroyo, 9, 19, 31–33, 53–55, 73, 76; Navern Covington, 45; Nancy Doniger, 37-39; Sherry Fissel, 96, 98; Meryl Henderson, 59, 66, 67; Loretta Lustig, 82, 83; Susan Nees, 35, 57; Jose Ortega, 108–115; Zina Saunders, 5, 72, 79, 85, 87–89, 91, 93, 95; Lauren Simeone, 68, 81, 100, 101; Susan Simon, 62, 69, 102; Matt Straub, 3, 27, 41, 58, 63, 77, 78, 90, 97, 103; Gerardo Suzan, 7, 13, 23, 25, 70

Macmillan/McGraw-Hill School Division
10 Union Square East
New York, New York 10003

Printed in the United States of America

ISBN 0-02-295169-5

 2 3 4 5 6 7 8 9 BAW 99 98 97 96 95

Contents

Contents

Introduction

Música para todos is a resource for both bilingual and monolingual classes. The materials are designed for use in a variety of teaching situations, including classes with:
- English-speaking students and students acquiring English as a second language;
- all Spanish-speaking students;
- all English-speaking students, who are acquiring Spanish as a second language.

Música para todos presents songs specially selected from the wealth of quality materials in *Share the Music* and includes the following key features:

- ***Spanish- and English-Language Songs:*** Musical materials include a selection of songs from both Spanish- and English-speaking cultures with singable translations This allows students, regardless of whether their first language is Spanish or English, to sing and enjoy favorite songs from each cultural heritage. All song pages are reproducible.

- ***Lesson Plans:*** Teaching suggestions promote musical concept and skill development and exploration of aspects of Hispanic and American culture. The use of the lesson plans requires no previous musical background.

- ***Visual Aids:*** Song Maps in the *Visual Aid* section are an innovative and effective tool in helping students develop Spanish and English vocabulary while reinforcing song lyrics. Additional visual resources include reproducible flashcards, manipulatives, and other tools to help motivate students and support teachers.

- ***Musical Script:*** The script combines selected Spanish- and English-language songs from *Música para todos* into a bilingual performance opportunity. Production, costume, and other performance notes are included.

- ***Teacher Talk:*** This resource section provides helpful suggestions for teachers working with students who are acquiring a second language—English or Spanish. Information is provided in a useful question-and-answer format. Translations for important musical and classroom terms and teaching phrases are included along with a Spanish pronunciation key.

- ***CD Recordings:*** All songs are recorded in both Spanish and English with culturally appropriate instrumentation. Pronunciation guides using the voices of native speakers are provided for all Spanish lyrics.

Organized to meet diverse teaching needs, *Música para todos* promotes cultural understanding and develops language skills for students of all backgrounds.

LA CUMBIA

Objective
Sing with pitch accuracy, diaphragmatic
   breathing, and appropriate diction

Materials
La cumbia **CD1:1**; Pronunciation **CD1:2**
Visual Aid M•1 (Song Map):
   prepare as transparency (optional)
tape recorder with blank cassette tape
Visual Aid M•2 (Vocal Development)
Visual Aid M•3 (Ostinato Overlay):
   prepare as transparency (optional)

TEACHING THE LESSON

1. **Introduce the song.** Have students:
   - Listen and decide what all the words you say have
     in common. (Name familiar dances: jitterbug,
     mambo, polka, cotton-eyed joe, twist, waltz.)
   - Mirror you as you lead some dances named.

2. **Teach the song.** Have students:
   - Listen to "La cumbia," a song about a Colombian
     dance, while following **Visual Aid M•1**.
   - Discuss the meaning of the words. (See
     Translation, below.)
   - Listen to and practice the pronunciation of the
     words while following the song map.

- Practice saying the vocabulary words listed on the
  board. (See **Vocabulary,** below.)
- Echo-sing and then sing the song.
- Record themselves as they sing the song.
- Listen to their tape and name any words that were
  hard to understand. (List these words on the board.)

3. **Teach the singing skills/assess
   learning.** Have students:
   - Look at the Body Position section of **Visual Aid
     M•2** and try the singing position. Freeze and check
     their positions for accuracy. Sing the song again and
     decide if their sound improved.
   - Practice the steps shown in the Breathing section of
     the Visual Aid. (Place hands on midsection; slowly
     inhale as hands separate from each other; slowly
     exhale until hands return to touching at midsection.)
   - Use the breathing and body position practiced while
     singing the song. Breathe only after *timbalero* and
     sol. Decide if they were better able to stay in tune.
   - Listen as you sing the vowels of the song, following
     the Vowels section of the Visual Aid. Sing the song
     only on the vowels.
   - Make a second recording of themselves singing,
     concentrating on body position, breathing, and
     vowel production. Compare the second recording
     with the first and decide which was easier to
     understand. Discuss why. (Better intonation,
     breathing, and vowels—list responses on board.)

RESOURCES

Vocal Ostinato
Have students add the following vocal
ostinato to "La cumbia." Have them
begin it on the downbeat as they
follow the song map. Lay **Visual Aid
M•3** over Visual Aid M•1 to show
how the ostinato goes with the song.

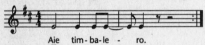

Aje tim-ba-le - ro.

Translation
The translation of "La cumbia" is
"Hey, Timbalero, dance the *cumbia* of
the sun."

Movement
1. Have students choose partners.
One partner holds a "candle" (mallet,
lummi stick, or unlit candle) while
moving forward with a shuffle step.
(A shuffle is a walk in which the feet
maintain contact with the ground.)
The other partner circles around the
first and gestures with a handkerchief
near the first partner's feet.
2. Have students make up their own
dance steps to the song.

Vocabulary
timbalero = drummer
baile = dance
cumbia = Colombian dance
sol = sun

Conversation Corner
*Hagan los movimientos que muestra el
   dibujo.* = Do the movement that
   the picture shows.
Ensayen estos sonidos. = Practice
   these sounds.
Vamos a grabar el ensayo. = Let's
   tape-record our singing.
*¿Qué grabación suena mejor, la
   primera o la segunda?* = Which
   sounded better, Recording 1 or 2?

Macmillan/McGraw-Hill

La cumbia

Popular Colombian Dance

Ai - e tim- ba- le - ro, bai - le cum- bia del sol.___ Ai -___

DON MARTÍN

Objective
Read and play rhythmic patterns

Materials
Don Martín: Spanish/English **CD1:3**;
  Pronunciation **CD1:4**
Visual Aid M•4 (Rhythm Patterns)
Visual Aid M•5 (Song Map)
four types of unpitched percussion instruments

TEACHING THE LESSON

1. **Prepare for the song.** Have students:
    • Echo-clap the patterns from **Visual Aid M•4.**
    • Clap each pattern without you, following the Visual Aid.
    • Clap the fourth pattern, adding these syllables:

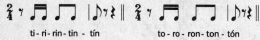

    ti - ri - rin - tin - tín   to - ro - ron - ton - tón

2. **Teach the song.** Have students:
    • Listen to "Don Martín," following **Visual Aid M•5** and signaling when they hear Pattern 4.

• Discuss the meaning of the song. (Don Martín's children die of measles.)
• Listen again, clapping and singing the pattern they have practiced when it occurs in the song.
• Listen to and practice the pronunciation of the song.
• Practice saying the vocabulary words listed on the board. (See **Vocabulary,** below.)
• Sing the song and clap the rhythm pattern at the appropriate times. Divide into two groups, one to clap on each *ti-ri-rin-tin-tín* as they sing, the other to clap on each *to-ro-ron-ton-tón.*

3. **Add instruments/assess learning.** Have students:
    • Form four groups, each group to play a different type of unpitched percussion instrument. (example: Group 1 plays rhythm sticks, Group 2 triangles, and so on.) Play the rhythm pattern they have practiced, each group assigned to a different phrase. (example: Group 1 plays it when it occurs in the first phrase, Group 2 when it occurs in the second phrase, and so on.)
    • Exchange instruments and/or assigned phrases.

RESOURCES

Playing Instruments
1. Let students experiment with different timbres by trying various instruments on *ti-ri-rin-tin-tín* and *to-ro-ron-ton-tón*. Encourage them to tell why they feel a particular instrument fits or does not fit the words.
2. Have students of each group select an instrument to imitate the sound of the words they have been assigned and take turns playing the pattern as they sing the song.
3. Have groups trade word patterns but not instruments. Ask the class to discuss the effect the change had on the way the song sounded.

Writing Notation
Challenge students to notate patterns you clap for them from the flashcards. Students can check their answers by identifying the correct flashcard.

Movement
Formation: partners
Move with each eighth note, starting on the first downbeat:
1. Hit own knees with both hands
2. Clap own hands
3. Partners clap right hands
4. Clap own hands
5. Partners clap left hands
6. Partners clap both hands
7. Partners touch backs of both hands
8. Partners clap both hands
Repeat the sequence, stopping when the singing ends.

Vocabulary
se le murió = it died on him
sarampión = measles

Conversation Corner
Avísenme cuando oigas el patrón.
  = Signal when you hear the pattern.
¿Por qué escogiste ese instrumento? =
  Why did you choose that instrument?

Don Martín

Mexican Folk Song
English Version by MMH

Spanish: A Don Mar - tín, ti - ri - rin - tin - tín, Se le mu -
English: Oh, Don Mar - tín, ti - ri - rin - tin - tín, His chil - dren

rió, to - ro - ron - ton - tón, Su chi - qui - tín, ti - ri - rin - tin -
cried, to - ro - ron - ton - tón, They got the mea - sles, ti - ri - rin - tin -

tín, De sa - ram - pión, to - ro - ron - ton - tón.
tín, And then they died! to - ro - ron - ton - tón.

ENTREN SANTOS PEREGRINOS
(Enter, Holy Pilgrims)

Objective
Perform an accompaniment using classroom
instruments

Materials
Entren santos peregrinos (Enter, Holy Pilgrims):
   Spanish/English **CD1:5**; Pronunciation **CD1:6**
Visual Aid M•6 (Song Map)
Visual Aid M•7 (Chord Roots)
resonator bells or Orff instruments (pitches D G
   A) one set for each small group
Visual Aid M•8 (Chords)

TEACHING THE LESSON

1. **Introduce the song.** Have students:
   - Share sentences people use when greeting guests at
     a door. (Hello, it's good to see you. Please come in.
     How are you? I'm glad you came.) Use Spanish
     greetings. (*Buenos días. ¿Cómo estás? Pasa.*)
   - Name things people do to help guests feel
     comfortable. (take their coats—*tomar sus abrigos*;
     invite them to sit down—*invitarles a sentarse*; offer
     them a beverage—*ofrecerles una bebida*)

2. **Teach the song.** Have students:
   - Listen to the song about some guests who are
     welcomed into a home, following **Visual Aid M•6**.
     Discuss the meaning of the words.
   - Listen to and practice the pronunciation of the
     words while following the Visual Aid.
   - Practice saying the vocabulary words listed on the
     board. (See **Vocabulary,** below.)
   - Echo-sing and then sing the song.

3. **Teach the accompaniment/assess
   learning.** Have students:
   - Look at **Visual Aid M•7** and say the letter names of
     the chord roots as you point to them.
   - Echo-sing the letter names.
   - Sing the letter names as you point to them while
     singing the song.
   - In groups of three or four, play pitches D G A on
     resonator bells or Orff instruments as the rest of the
     students sing the song. Change players after each
     verse until each student has had a turn playing.

RESOURCES

Playing Chords
Have students play the full chords
using **Visual Aid M•8**. Additional
resonator bells needed are F♯ B C♯ D E.

Dramatization
Have students create a pathway in the
room using classroom objects,
instruments, or furniture as the
outline of the pathway. Have them
work in small groups to dramatize the
words of the song. They may use the
song map to generate ideas. Ask each
group to practice and perform their
dramatization for the class while
walking down the pathway.

Vocabulary
peregrinos = pilgrims
corazón = heart

Conversation Corner
¿Cómo dice la gente, "Hola"? = How
   do people say, "Hello"?
Canten estos sonidos. = Sing these
   sounds.
Lean y toquen. = Read and play.
Representen las palabras. = Dramatize
   the words.

Entren santos peregrinos

(Enter, Holy Pilgrims)

Mexican Folk Song
English Version by MMH

Spanish: En - tren san - tos pe - re - gri - nos, pe - re - gri - nos,— Re - ci -
English: En - ter in, all ho - ly pil - grims, ho - ly pil - grims.— Wel - come

ban es - te rin - cón, que aun - que es po - bre la mo - ra - da, la mo -
to our hum - ble grove. There is lit - tle we can give you, we can

ra - da,— Os la doy de co - ra - zón.
give you,— Still we wel - come you with love.

DE ALLACITO CARNAVALITO
(The Carnival Is Coming)

Objective
Move to music

Materials
De allacito carnavalito (The Carnival Is Coming):
    Spanish/English **CD1:7**; Pronunciation **CD1:8**
Visual Aid M•9 (Worksheet)
Visual Aid M•10 (Song Map)
Visual Aid M•11 (Cue Cards): prepare one set

TEACHING THE LESSON

1. **Introduce the song.** Have students:
    • Use **Visual Aid M•9** and list places they like to go with another person. Make another list of things they like to do alone. (Tell them a Spanish word for *partner* is *pareja*, one for *alone* is *solito.)*

2. **Teach the song.** Have students:
    • Listen to "De allacito carnavalito," following **Visual Aid M•10**, and signal when they hear the Spanish words *pareja* and *solito.*
    • Discuss the meaning of the song. (It's about going to a carnival.)
    • Listen to and practice the pronunciation of the song.

• Practice saying the vocabulary words listed on the board. (See **Vocabulary**, below.)
• Echo-sing, then sing the song, following the song map.
• Relate their list of things they do with other people to the meaning of the song.
• Sing the song again, adding gestures on *pareja* (hold up two fingers) and *solito* (hold up an index finger).

3. **Move to the song/assess learning.** Have students:
    • Practice the movements from **Visual Aid M•11.**
    • Form two long lines, partners facing each other.
    • Clap their partner's hands with the beat as they sing the first phrase of the song, repeating as indicated.
    • Continue singing while, on the second phrase of the song, the student at the head of Line 1 goes to the *carnavalito* alone. (The student draws a card from the pile of movement cue cards, then performs that movement down the "aisle" for the eight beats of Phrase 2, ending up in a new position at the foot of Line 1. Students will have new partners each time they sing the song. Repeat the song until all in Line 1 have had a turn to perform *solito*. Give those in Line 2 a chance to perform on another occasion.)

RESOURCES

Playing Instruments
Have students play the melody of Phrase 1 of the song on recorders.

Creating Movement
Have students repeat the movement activity, letting partners create movements to do together as they move down the aisle.

Vocabulary
carnavalito = little carnival
pareja = partner
solito = alone

Conversation Corner
¿Qué les gusta hacer con otra persona? = What do you like to do with another person?
¿Qué les gusta hacer solos(as)? = What do you like to do by yourself?
Hagan dos líneas. = Make two lines.
Pónganse enfrente de sus parejas. = Face your partners.
¿Cómo te moverás por el pasillo? = How will you move down the aisle?

Macmillan/McGraw-Hill

De allacito carnavalito
(The Carnival Is Coming)

Argentine Folk Song
English Version by MMH

Spanish: De a-lla-ci-to, de a-lla-ci-to, ya vie-ne el car-na-va-li-to;
English: Ev'-ry-one there is— com-ing down to the *car-na-va-li-to.*

To-dos ba-jan en pa-re-ja, yo voy ba-jan-do so-li-to.
Ev'-ry-one comes down in cou-ples, I am a lone-ly— so-lo.

ALEGRÍA, ALEGRÍA
(Joy, Joy)

Objective
Create a dramatization to music

Materials
Alegría, alegría (Joy, Joy): Spanish/English **CD1:9**;
  Pronunciation **CD1:10**
Visual Aid M•12 (Worksheet)
Visual Aid M•13 (Song Map)
classroom objects, instruments, or furniture that
  can be used to border a walking path
Visual Aid M•14 (Flashcards), one set for each
  small group (optional)

TEACHING THE LESSON

1. **Introduce the song.** Have students:
   - Imagine they are traveling with their best friend to visit some friends in a nearby town, then use **Visual Aid M•12** to illustrate their responses to questions such as:
       Who do you see along the way?
       What types of scenery do you see?
       What kind of traffic and vehicles pass by?

2. **Teach the song.** Have students:
   - Listen to "Alegría, alegría," following **Visual Aid M•13**.
   - Discuss the meaning of the words. (*María*/Mary and *su esposo*/Joseph are traveling to *Belén*/Bethlehem.)
   - Compare the things they described above with the story of the song. (See Step 1 above.)
   - Listen to and practice the pronunciation of the words while following the song map.
   - Practice saying the vocabulary words listed on the board. (See **Vocabulary,** below.)
   - Echo-sing, then sing the song.

3. **Create a dramatization/assess learning.** Have students:
   - Form small groups with at least four members. Within each group, decide who will represent Mary, Joseph, and other people along the pathway who greet them. Make up a dramatization of the trip to *Belén*. Practice their roles while singing the song.
   - Use classroom objects, instruments, or furniture to create a pathway through which each group will be able to walk. As the entire class sings the song, each group performs its dramatization while walking down the pathway.

RESOURCES

Singing in Small Groups
For practice singing in small groups, have each group perform its dramatization for the first three lines of the song while singing from *Hacia* through *poderoso*. Have the rest of the class join in on *Alegría* and sing with the group to the end of the song.

Playing Instruments
Have students accompany the song by playing the roots of the chords shown above the notation. Some may play the full chords on resonator bells, guitars, or autoharps.

Reading Notation
Assist students as they study **Visual Aid M•14** to learn the names and functions of some elements of musical notation from the song. In small groups, they may drill each other on locating and naming each symbol. Finally, have individual students point out each symbol on a transparency of the song as you name it. Have the other students signal with thumbs up if they agree with the answer given or thumbs down if they do not.

Vocabulary
Belén = Bethlehem
esposo = husband
alegría = happiness
placer = pleasure

Conversation Corner
Vamos a representar. = Let's pretend.
Representen la canción. = Dramatize the song.
Anden por la vereda. = Walk down the path.

Alegría, alegría
(Joy, Joy)

Puerto Rican Folk Song
English Version by MMH

CHÍU, CHÍU, CHÍU

Objective

Perform an accompaniment using unpitched
instruments

Materials

Chíu, chíu, chíu: Spanish/English **CD1:11**;
  Pronunciation **CD1:12**
Visual Aid M•15 (Song Map):
  prepare as transparency (optional)
transparency markers (optional)
Visual Aid M•16 (Flashcards): one set
supplies for making flashcards (optional)
unpitched percussion instruments

TEACHING THE LESSON

1. **Introduce the song.** Have students:
    *   Make the sound of a rooster. (cock-a-doodle-doo)
    *   Name other kinds of birds and make the sound for
        each. (crow = caw, dove = coo, duck = quack,
        and so on)
    *   Give some examples of Spanish bird songs. (Baby
        chicks or *pollitos* sing *pío, pío, pío*, and roosters or
        gallos sing *qui qui ri quí*.)
    *   Discover that not all birds make the same sound,
        yet all can "sing."

2. **Teach the song.** Have students:
    *   Listen to the song, following **Visual Aid M•15**, and
        determine what song the *pajarito* sings. (*chíu, chíu,
        chíu, chíu*)

*   Look for lines in the song in which words are the
    same, similar, or different. Highlight or underline
    those that are the same with a transparency marker
    or on individual copies of the Visual Aid. (same:
    lyrics of mm. 1-2 and 13-14, mm. 6-8 and 14-16, and
    Phrases 1 and 2 of refrain)
*   Listen to and practice the pronunciation of the song.
*   Practice saying the vocabulary words listed on the
    board. (See **Vocabulary**, below.)
*   Practice the bird songs from **Visual Aid M•16**, then
    create flashcards for other bird songs.
*   Listen to the song again, adding a bird song at the
    end of each phrase.
*   Echo-sing, then sing the song, following the song map.

3. **Add instruments/assess learning.** Have
    students:
    *   Select an instrument to represent each of four birds
        from the flashcards.
    *   Set up four groups, each assigned a bird, and
        prepare to take turns within each group playing the
        selected instrument.
    *   Sing the song, playing with the beat only when they
        see the flashcard with their bird. (Show a new card
        with each phrase of the song.)
    *   Select different bird songs and different instruments
        for additional performances.

RESOURCES

Vocal Exploration

Let students explore with their own
voices the two types of bird songs
mentioned in the refrain, *gorjeos*
(warbling, chirping) and *trinar* (trill).
Show them the musical symbol for a
trill (*tr* ⌣) and discuss how the
human voice can imitate a bird's trill.

Vocabulary

canta = sing
pajarito = little bird
triste = sad
me alegra = makes me happy
corazón = heart

Conversation Corner

*¿Pueden hacer el sonido de un
  pájaro?* = Can you make a bird
  sound?
*¿Pueden hacer los sonidos de otros
  pájaros?* = Can you make the
  sounds of other birds?
¿Cómo canta este pájaro? = How
  does this bird sing?

Macmillan/McGraw-Hill

Chíu, chíu, chíu

Uruguayan Folk Song
English Version by MMH

Estrofa/Verse

Spanish: Can - ta, can - ta, pa - ja - ri - to.____ Can - ta, can - ta tu can -
English: *Can - ta, can - ta pa - ja - ri - to.____* Sing the songs that cheer me

ción, Mi - ra que la vi - da es tris - te y tu can -
so. See, my life is full of sor - row, your mer - ry

tar me a - le - gra el co - ra - zón. Chí - u, chí - u, chí - u,
sing - ing sets my heart a - glow. *Chí - u, chí - u, chí - u,*

chí - u,____ chí - u, chí - u, chí - u, chí - u.____ Can - ta, can - ta pa - ja-
chí - u,____ chí - u, chí - u, chí - u, chí - u.____ Can - ta, can - ta pa - ja-

ri - to. Que tu can - tar me a - le - gra el co - ra - zón.
ri - to. Your mer - ry sing - ing sets my heart a - glow.

CHÍU, CHÍU, CHÍU   PAGE 2

Estribillo/Refrain

Con tus gor - je - os,—— con tu tri - nar,   Des - pier - ta el
Your mer - ry   chirp - ing;—— your roun - de - lay,   You bring   the

al - ba, la no - che ya se va.   Con tus gor - je - os,——con tu tri-
dawn - ing, the shad - ows fade a - way,   Your mer - ry chirp - ing;—your roun - de-

nar,——   Des - pier - ta el   al - ba, la no - che ya se va.
lay.——   You bring   the   dawn - ing, the shad - ows fade a - way.

EL QUELITE
(The Village)

Objective
Play a chordal accompaniment on guitar or autoharp

Materials
El quelite (The Village): Spanish/English **CD1:13**;
   Pronunciation **CD1:14**
Visual Aid M•17 (Song Map):
   prepare as transparency (optional)
transparency of song "El quelite" (optional)
transparency markers of three different colors
   (optional)
guitars or autoharps (one for every two students)
Visual Aid M•18 (Ostinato)

TEACHING THE LESSON

1. **Introduce the song.** Have students:
   • Look at **Visual Aid M•17** for 10 to 15 seconds, then take turns naming as much as they can remember of what they saw. (Make a list on the board: Mexican village scene; man with serape and hat, carrying bucket; donkey pulling cart; man moving barrel; woman in cart; woman hanging wash; rooster crowing; sign pointing out of village.)
   • Look at the Visual Aid again to see how much they recalled and what they missed.

   • Decide where they could travel to see a place like the one depicted. (Mexican village, the country)

2. **Teach the song.** Have students:
   • Listen to "El quelite" while following the song map.
   • Discuss the meaning of the words. (A traveler wants to be remembered.)
   • Listen to and practice the pronunciation of the words while following the song map.
   • Practice saying the vocabulary words listed on the board. (See **Vocabulary,** below.)
   • Echo-sing, then sing the song.

3. **Introduce instrumental parts/assess learning.** Have students:
   • Look at the song and watch as you point to or use a different color to highlight each chord. (example: Use green = D, orange = A7, blue = G.)
   • Form small groups and take turns having group members sing the song or speak the chord names until each member has had a chance to do both.
   • Take turns singing the song and playing the chords on a guitar or autoharp.
   • Share instruments among groups as necessary to allow all the members of each group to play at the same time. Perform and sing for the other groups. Rotate the instruments from group to group until all groups have performed for each other.

RESOURCES

Ostinato
1. Have some students sing and clap this ostinato while others sing the melody:

Ma- ña-na me voy, ma - ña-na me voy.

2. Have students read the ostinato from **Visual Aid M•18** and play it on resonator bells or Orff instruments while others sing the song. Have them tap mallet handles for the claps.

Movement
Formation: two concentric circles, facing each other, eight steps apart, with boys inside, girls outside.
Step with the dotted-quarter-note beat.
   Measures 1-16: Move four steps toward partner; three steps back away. Clap ♪♩ after last step. Repeat sequence four times, through *ajena.*
   Measures 17-24: At *Mañana, me voy,* all turn and circle to their right, stepping with the beat. (Circles move in opposite directions.) After last word, all stop, face a new partner, and clap the ♪♩ rhythm.
Repeat with the new partner.

Vocabulary
me dio sueño = I fall asleep
me despertó = it awoke me
mañana = tomorrow
me voy = I'm leaving

Conversation Corner
¿Qué recuerdan del retrato? = What do you remember about the picture?
Canten. = Sing.
Toquen estos sonidos. = Play these sounds.
Toquen la guitarra o el autoharp. = Play the guitar or autoharp.

Macmillan/McGraw-Hill

El quelite

(The Village)

Mexican Folk Song
English Version by MMH

Spanish: Al pie de un ver-de que-li-te me dio sue-ño y me dor-
English: At the edge of a green— que-li-te, I stopped a-while there to

mí, y me des-per-tó un ga-lli-to can-tan-do "qui qui ri
sleep. A roos-ter cried out and woke me. He sang a "qui qui ri

quí." Yo no can-to por-que sí pue-do, ni por-que mi voz se-a
quí." I don't sing be-cause I'm a-ble, nor be-cause— my voice is

bue-na, can-to por-que ten-go gu-sto en mi tie-rra y en la a-
good.— I sing be-cause I feel joy— in my land— and for-eign

je-na. Ma-ña-na, me voy ma-ña-na, ma-ña-na me voy de a-
lands.— To-mor-row I will be leav-ing, and who can tell where I'll

quí, y el con-sue-lo que me que-da que se han de a-cor-dar de mi.
be? But here is my con-so-la-tion: that some-one re-mem-bers me.

SI ME DAN PASTELES
(When You Bring Pasteles)

Objective
Sing short sections of a song in small groups and
as solos

Materials
Si me dan pasteles (When You Bring *Pasteles*):
Spanish/English **CD1:15**; Pronunciation **CD1:16**;
Performance Mix **CD1:17**
Visual Aid M•19 (Worksheet)
Visual Aid M•20 (Song Map)
Visual Aid M•21 (Word Cards): one set for each
pair of students
transparency of song (optional)
transparency markers of two colors (optional)

TEACHING THE LESSON

1. **Introduce the song.** Have students:
    *   Create a menu for their favorite holiday meal.
        (Suggest Christmas, Thanksgiving, Fourth of July,
        and so on.) Discuss the courses using **Visual Aid
        M•19.**
    *   Listen as you read the background for the song.
        (See **Background,** below.)

2. **Teach the song.** Have students:
    *   Listen to "Si me dan pasteles," following **Visual Aid
        M•20.** Pay particular attention to the words they
        hear when you point to the pictures on the song map.

*   Listen to and practice the pronunciation of the song.
*   Practice the vocabulary words listed on the board.
    (See **Vocabulary,** below.)
*   Choose partners and use **Visual Aid M•21** to
    determine the Spanish word for each picture shown
    on the song map. Place the word cards in the order
    found in the song. Listen to the song again to confirm
    the order.
*   Echo-sing, then sing the song, following the song
    map.
*   Look at the song (Part 1) and identify two pairs
    of melodic phrases that are the same or similar.
    (Phrases 1, 3; Phrases 2, 4) Mark the pairs of
    phrases using two different colors.

3. **Sing in groups and as solos/assess learning.**
    Have students:
    *   Divide into two groups and sing an assigned part of
        the song. (Group 1, for example could be assigned
        to sing Phrase 1 and identify and sing the other
        phrase that has the same melody—Phrase 3. Group
        2 could be assigned to sing Phrase 2 and the phrase
        that is similar to its melody—Phrase 4).
    *   Sing the entire song, each group singing its assigned
        part. Sing in unison on the interlude.
    *   Divide into groups of four and assign each member
        one phrase. Each soloist performs in turn. Exchange
        phrases for subsequent performances.

RESOURCES

Playing Instruments
Have students play the melody on
recorders or on resonator bells
F# G A B C.

Singing Harmony
Have students learn Parts 2 and 3
separately. When they are secure in
singing each part, have them practice
Parts 2 and 3 together, then sing the
song with all three parts.

Background
"Si me dan pasteles" is traditionally
sung during the Christmas season,
especially around January 6, Three
Kings Day (Epiphany). The song is
often sung by strolling carolers, and
listeners offer them holiday delicacies
such as *pasteles. Pasteles* are a
combination of cooked plantain and
meat made into patties and wrapped
in plantain leaves. Some fill them with
rice or other fillers. The Christmas
dinner, eaten after Midnight Mass,
often begins with *pasteles* as well.

Vocabulary
pasteles = meat and plantain patties
calientes = hot ones
fríos = cold ones
arroz = rice
cuchara = spoon

Conversation Corner
*Relacionen cada palabra con el
    dibujo que le corresponda.* –
    Match the word to its picture.
¿A qué se parece el bananero? =
    What does a plantain look like?

Macmillan/McGraw-Hill

Si me dan pasteles
(When You Bring *Pasteles*)

Puerto Rican Folk Song
Arranged by Alejandro Jiménez
English Version by MMH

World Music Press for *Si me dan pasteles*. Traditional Puerto Rican aguinaldo arranged by Alejandro Jiménez.
© 1986 Alejandro Jiménez/World Music Press, P.O. Box 2565, Danbury, CT 06813.
Used by permission.

Macmillan/McGraw-Hill

SI ME DAN PASTELES (When You Bring *Pasteles*) PAGE 2

Si me dan a - rroz___ no me den cu - cha - ra,___
If you give me rice ones,___ don't give me *cu - cha - ra,*___

Le lo lai, le lo lai,

que ma - má me di - jo___ que se lo lle - va - ra.___
My *ma - má* has told me___ "Bring them straight home to me!"___

le lo lai, le lo lai.

Interludio/Interlude

Le lo lai, le lo lai. Le lo lai, le lo lai.

Le lo lai, le lo lai. Le lo lai, le lo lai.

CAMPANAS VESPERTINAS
(Evening Bells)

Objective
Perform a chordal accompaniment using autoharp or keyboard

Materials
Campanas vespertinas (Evening Bells):
  Spanish/English **CD1:18**; Pronunciation **CD1:19**;
  Performance Mix **CD1:20**
resonator bell
Visual Aid M•22 (Song Map)
Visual Aid M•23 (Chords)
autoharps or keyboards (one to every pair of students)

TEACHING THE LESSON

1. **Introduce the song.** Have students:
   - Close their eyes and listen as you play one pitch on a resonator bell. Name the time of day the instrument is announcing by counting the number of times it plays. (Play 12, 6, and 8 chimes.)
   - Decide what a person might be doing at those times. (12 noon/midnight—eating lunch/sleeping, 6 A.M./P.M.—waking up/eating dinner, 8 A.M./P.M.—going to school/doing homework)
   - Listen as one student strikes another time of day and describe what they do at that time.

2. **Teach the song.** Have students:
   - Listen to "Campanas vespertinas," following **Visual Aid M•22**.
   - Discuss the meaning of the words. (They describe evening church bells ringing.)
   - Listen to and practice the pronunciation of the words while following the song map.
   - Practice saying the vocabulary words listed on the board. (See **Vocabulary,** below.)
   - Echo-sing, then sing the melody.

3. **Teach the accompaniment/assess learning.**
   Have students:
   - Look at **Visual Aid M•23** and say the chord names written above the staff as you point to them.
   - Echo-sing, then sing the chord names on the chord root pitches.
   - Form two groups and take turns singing the melody and the chord names.
   - Work in pairs, one partner singing and the other playing chord roots or full chords on autoharp or keyboard. Switch parts.

RESOURCES

Movement
Formation: Two lines of 4-6 couples standing side by side; boys holding wrists behind backs, girls pretending to hold a fan in one hand and the hem of a full skirt in the other
Mexican-Style Waltz Step:
Practice a gentle shuffle-step: step, close, step. Couples sway toward each other, starting with the inside foot on first beat of the pattern, and then away from each other, starting with the outside foot on the next pattern.
Measures 1-4: Head couple separates, leading each line to the foot of the set, for four waltz steps.

Measures 5-8: Head couple leads diagonally across the space of the set; boys passing behind partners, and all waltzing down the outside of the set to meet partners at the foot.
Measures 9-16: Return to the original position. Exchange places with partner, passing right shoulders.

Playing Instruments
Have some students read and play the accompaniment part from the staff notation while others sing and dance. (See **Movement,** above.)

Singing Harmony
Have students learn the harmony part. When they are secure with singing each part separately, have them sing both parts together.

Vocabulary
campanas = bells
iglesia = church
qué dulce = how sweet
corazón = heart

Conversation Corner
¿Qué hora es? = What time is it?
Digan estas letras. = Say these letters.
Hagan turnos. = Take turns.

Macmillan/McGraw-Hill

Campanas vespertinas

(Evening Bells)

Music by Julio Z. Guerra
Words by Juana Guglielmi
English Version by MMH

Andante

Spanish: Las cam - pa - nas de la i - gle - sia dan el to - que de o - ra - ción
English: Hear the ring - ing of the church bells, hear them call - ing, hear the sound.

Y la luz del sol que mue - re a o-tro mun - do i - rá a a - lum - brar.
See the sun- light slow-ly dy - ing, as the eve - ning comes a - round.

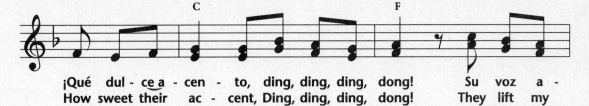

¡Qué dul - ce a - cen - to, ding, ding, ding, dong! Su voz a -
How sweet their ac - cent, Ding, ding, ding, dong! They lift my

D.C. Heath and Company for *Campanas vespertinas*
by Julio Z. Guerra and Juana Gugliemi from MASTERING MUSIC, 6th GRADE.
Reprinted by permission of D.C. Heath and Company.

CAMPANAS VESPERTINAS   (Evening Bells)   PAGE 2

le - gra mi co - ra - zón.   ¡Ding ding ding dong!
heart with their e - ven - song.   Ding ding ding dong!

le - gra mi co - ra - zón.   ¡Ding ding ding
heart with their e - ven - song.   Ding ding ding

Su voz a - le - gra mi co - ra - zón.
They lift my heart With their e - ven - song.

dong!   Ay, mi co - ra - zón.
dong!   With their e - ven - song.

DE COLORES
(Many Colors)

Objective
Create movement to music

Materials
De colores (Many Colors): Spanish **CD1:21**;
   Pronunciation **CD1:22**; English **CD1:23**
Visual Aid M•24 (Song Map): make transparency
transparency markers of various colors
Visual Aid M•25 (Flashcards): one set
streamers of various colors, one for each student
   (Make from crepe paper strips, plastic surveyor's
   tape, scarves, or ribbons.)
construction paper of various colors
   (See **Making Cue Cards,** below; make one set.)

TEACHING THE LESSON

1. **Introduce the song.** Have students:
   - Name the four seasons. (spring—*primavera*,
     summer—*verano,* fall—*otoño,* winter—*invierno*)
   - Name some signs of spring (flowers growing, new
     leaves on trees, birds singing, green grass), then list
     colors that remind them of spring.

2. **Teach the song.** Have students:
   - Listen to "De colores," following verse one on
     Visual Aid M•24 and swaying with the beat.
   - Discuss the song's use. (See **Background,** below.)
   - Listen to and practice the pronunciation of the song.
   - Practice saying the vocabulary words listed on the
     board. (See **Vocabulary,** below.)
   - Echo-sing the song, then sing it, following the song
     map and noticing the colors of the phrases. (See
     Coloring the Song Map, below.)

3. **Teach the movement/assess learning.** Have
   students:
   - Name the color of each streamer in both English
     and Spanish, using **Visual Aid M•25**. (Streamers
     may not match the song map and cue cards,
     depending on materials used.)
   - Practice the movements with their streamers. (See
     Making Cue Cards, with illustration, below.)
   - Sing the song and move their streamers as indicated
     by the cue card you hold up. (Phrase 1 = Card 1,
     and so on; repeated phrase = Card 4.)
   - Create new streamer movements on their own.

RESOURCES

Background
"De colores" is a popular song and a
symbol of Mexican heritage. It
became a theme song for Mexican
Americans striving for fair treatment
in the United States in the 1970s. The
song was used by farm workers led by
Cesar Chavez and by *Raza Unida,*
United People, another group working
for civil rights. *Many colors* came to
mean equality of all races.

Movement
1. Let a student lead the activity.
2. Have small groups design their
own sequence of cue cards. Have
them sing and perform for the class.

Making Cue Cards
Draw each figure shown on a piece of
construction paper, matching the color
of paper to the colors of the song map.

Front circle to right   Front circle to left

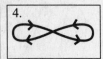

Rainbow over head   Figure eight

Coloring the Song Map
Outline with a different color the
section of ribbon for each song
phrase. Match each phrase to the
color of the cue card for that phrase.
Use contrasting colors to decorate.

Vocabulary
colores = colors
primavera = spring
pajarillos = birds
arco iris = rainbow
me gustan a mí = I like it

Conversation Corner
¿Qué ocurre en primavera? = What
   happens in spring?
*¿Qué colores les recuerdan a la
   primavera?* = What colors remind
   you of spring?
¿De qué color es su bandolera? = What
   color is your streamer?

Macmillan/McGraw-Hill

De colores
(Many Colors)

Spanish Folk Song
English Version by MMH

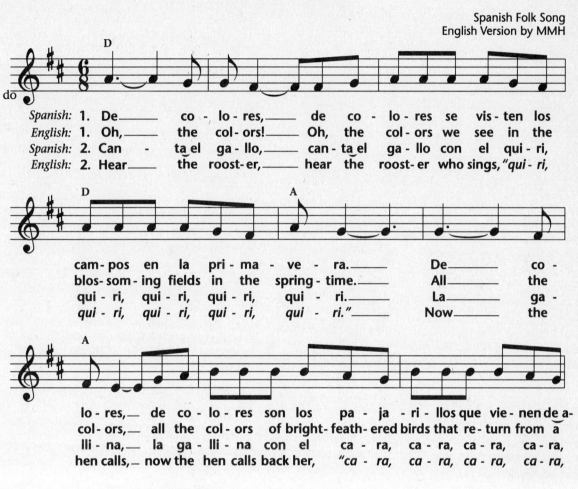

Spanish: 1. De_____ co - lo - res,___ de co - lo - res se vis - ten los
English: 1. Oh,___ the col - ors!___ Oh, the col - ors we see in the
Spanish: 2. Can - ta el ga - llo,___ can - ta el ga - llo con el qui - ri,
English: 2. Hear___ the roost - er,___ hear the roost - er who sings, "qui - ri,

cam - pos en la pri - ma - ve - ra.___ De_____ co -
blos - som - ing fields in the spring - time.___ All___ the
qui - ri, qui - ri, qui - ri, qui - ri.___ La ga -
*qui - ri, qui - ri, qui - ri, qui - ri."*___ Now___ the

lo - res,__ de co - lo - res son los pa - ja - ri - llos que vie - nen de a-
col - ors,__ all the col - ors of bright- feath- ered birds that re- turn from a
lli - na, la ga - lli - na con el ca - ra, ca - ra, ca - ra, ca - ra,
hen calls,__ now the hen calls back her, *"ca - ra, ca - ra, ca - ra, ca - ra,*

DE COLORES   (Many Colors)   PAGE 2

D

fue - ra._____ De_____ co - lo - res,_____ de co -
dis - tance._____ Oh,_____ the col - ors!_____ Oh, the
ca - ra._____ Los_____ po - llue - los,_____ los po -
*ca - ra."*_____ Hear_____ the small ones,_____ Hear the

D   G

lo - res es el ar - co i - ris que ve - mos lu - cir._____ Y por
col - ors that light up the sky in a beau - ti - ful rain - bow!_____ And the
llue - los con el pí - o, pí - o, pí - o, pí - o, pí - o._____ Y por
small ones cry out, *"pí - o, pí - o, pí - o, pí - o, pí - o."*_____ And the

G   D

e - so los gran - des a - mo - res de mu - chos co -
col - ors of true love are bright - est, and these are the

1.   2.
A   D   A7   D

lo - res me gus - tan a mí._____ Y por lo - res me gus - tan a mí.
col - ors I love most of all._____ And the col - ors I love most of all.

ENGLISH-LANGUAGE SONGS **Lesson 1**

FOR THY GRACIOUS BLESSINGS/
FOR HEALTH AND STRENGTH
(Por sus bendiciones/Salud y fuerza)

Objective
Compose an interlude and sing two rounds

Materials
For Thy Gracious Blessings (Por sus bendiciones):
 Spanish **CD1:24**; Pronunciation **CD1:25**; English
 CD1:26; Performance Mix **CD1:27**
For Health and Strength (Salud y fuerza): Spanish
 CD1:28; Pronunciation **CD1:29**; English **CD1:30**
Visual Aid M•26 (Song Maps): prepare as two
 transparencies (optional)
pencil (or transparency pointer)
unpitched percussion instruments

TEACHING THE LESSON

1. **Introduce the songs.** Have students:
    *   List on the board some holidays and name a song
        for each. (examples: Christmas–"Jingle Bells";
        Fourth of July–"Yankee Doodle") Consider which
        holidays are celebrated only in the United States.
    *   Listen as you tell them that today they will learn
        two songs associated with Thanksgiving, a
        traditional holiday in the United States. Discuss the
        fact that people of many cultures and countries have
        special days for giving thanks.

2. **Teach the songs.** Have students:
    *   Listen to "For Thy Gracious Blessings," following
        Visual Aid M•26. (Rotate the Visual Aid to follow
        the words; use a pencil as a stationary pointer.)
    *   Listen to and practice the pronunciation for the
        song.
    *   Practice saying the vocabulary words listed on the
        board. (See **Vocabulary**, below.)
    *   Echo-sing, then sing the song in unison, following
        the Visual Aid.
    *   Perform the song as a two-part round, with the class
        singing Part 1 as you sing Part 2.
    *   Divide into two groups and perform the round.
    *   Use the same steps for "For Health and Strength."
    *   Compare and contrast the two rounds by looking at
        the two song maps on Visual Aid M•26. (Lay the
        two song transparencies one over the other.) Notice
        the length (one is longer), the subject (both give
        thanks), and the entry points for Part 2.

3. **Compose an interlude/assess learning.** Have
    students:
    *   Determine which song will be A and which B.
    *   Compose a four-measure interlude on unpitched
        instruments to perform between sections of the
        composition. Use rhythms from both songs.
    *   Perform the songs in this form: Song A (as a
        round), Interlude, Song B (as a round).

RESOURCES

Movement
1. Have students learn the movement
for "For Health and Strength."
   Formation: two lines facing
(Verbal Cue–*forward, close,
backward, close; turn, 2, 3, 4*)
Step R foot forward on *health*, close L
foot beside R on *strength*, step R foot
backward on *daily*, close L foot next
to R on *food*. Turn once in place on
We praise Thy name, stop on *Lord*.

Final Form: Decide which line will
start in the canon, then perform the
step while singing, first in unison,
then in canon. (The unison and canon
floor patterns will differ.)
2. Create movement for "For Thy
Gracious Blessings."
3. Add movement to the form created
in the lesson above. Perform Song A's
movement by itself as an Introduction
and Song B's movement as a Coda.

Vocabulary
bendiciones = blessings
voluntad = wishes
gracias = thanks
salud = health
fuerza = strength
alimento = daily food
Dios = Lord

Conversation Corner
*Les haré una señal para que empiecen
 a cantar.* = I will signal when it's
 your turn to begin singing.

Música para todos **for Intermediate Grades**

For Thy Gracious Blessings
(Por sus bendiciones)

Traditional Melody
Arranged by Marilyn C. Davidson
English Words by Lester S. Bucher
Spanish Version by MMH

Discante/Descant

Spanish: Por sus ben - di - cio - nes,
English: For Thy gra - cious bless - ings,

Melodía/Melody

Spanish: Por sus ben - di - cio - nes,
English: For Thy gra - cious bless - ings,

Por su ca - ri - dad,
For Thy won - drous Word,

Por su ca - ri - dad,
For Thy won - drous Word,

FOR THY GRACIOUS BLESSINGS   (Por sus bendiciones)   PAGE 2

Por   su   vo - lun - tad,   Le
For   Thy   lov - ing kind - ness,

Por   su   bue - na   vo - lun - tad,   Le
For   Thy   lov - ing   kind - ness,____ Le

da -   mos   gra -   cias.
We   give   thanks,   Oh   Lord.

da - mos   gra -   cias.
We   give   thanks,   Oh   Lord.

For Health and Strength

(Salud y fuerza)

Old English Round
Spanish Version by MMH

Spanish: Sa - lud y fuer - za, a - li - men -
English: For health and strength and dai - ly food

to: Da - mos gra - cias Dios.
We praise Thy name, Oh, Lord.

I LOVE THE MOUNTAINS
(Amo las montañas)

Objective
Read and perform a rhythmic accompaniment

Materials
I Love the Mountains (Amo las montañas):
  Spanish **CD2:1**; Pronunciation **CD2:2**; English
  CD2:3
Visual Aid M•27 (Song Map)
Visual Aid M•28 (Rhythm Patterns): prepare as
  transparency (optional); mount each pattern on
  construction paper as a sign
transparency marking pen (optional)
unpitched percussion instruments (Use enough
  instruments for all students to play at once. Put
  rhythm sticks in one location in the room,
  woodblocks in another, and drums in a third.
  Use a rhythm pattern sign for each location.)

TEACHING THE LESSON

1. **Introduce the song.** Have students:
   - Imagine they are going to camp out and decide what
     to take, where to go, what to eat, and so on.
   - Sit in a circle as if around a warm campfire. Name
     some things they saw and did in their day outdoors.

2. **Teach the song.** Have students:
   - Listen to "I Love the Mountains," following **Visual
     Aid M•27.** Discuss the meaning of the words.
   - Listen to and practice the pronunciation for the
     words while following Visual Aid M•27.
   - Practice saying the vocabulary words listed on the
     board. (See **Vocabulary,** below.)
   - Echo-sing, then sing the song.

3. **Introduce the rhythmic accompaniment/
   assess learning.** Have students:
   - Alternate hands as they tap the rhythm of the words
     on their legs and sing the song.
   - Look at three rhythm patterns used in the song on
     Visual Aid M•28. Tap and say the words in rhythm.
   - Look at Visual Aid M•27 and circle each *Amo las
     montañas* rhythm pattern, draw a rectangle around
     each *Amo los narcisos* rhythm pattern, and put a
     wiggly line around each *Bum-di-a-da, Bum-di-a-da*
     rhythm pattern. Use Visual Aid M•28 as a guide or
     to check their responses.
   - Notice that Measures 3 and 6 of the song don't
     match any of the patterns exactly, and decide to
     which patterns they are most similar. (Measure 3
     —Pattern 1; Measure 6—Pattern 2)
   - Divide into three groups, one for each set of
     instruments in the room. Sing the song and play
     their assigned pattern when it occurs. After
     performing the song once, move to the next rhythm
     pattern and set of instruments and perform again.
     Continue moving and singing until every student
     has played all three rhythm patterns.

RESOURCES

Practicing Rhythms
Have individual students choose a
rhythm pattern and perform it.

Singing in Parts
1. Have students sing the song as a
three-part canon.
2. Have them sing in parts, with one
group singing *Bum-di-a-da, Bum-di-
a-da* as an ostinato and another group
singing the other phrases.
3. Select soloists for each of the
phrases while the rest of the class
sings the *Bum-di-a-da* ostinato.

Creating Gestures
Have students agree on expressive
gestures for key words of the song.
The gestures can be performed in
canon or in parts, according to how
the song is performed.

ABA Form
Have students perform in ABA form:
sing the song, play the rhythm of the
song, sing again.

Vocabulary
montañas = mountains
flores = flowers
hoguera = bonfire
luz = light

Conversation Corner
*Siéntense en el piso formando un
  círculo.* = Form a circle and sit on
  the floor.
Finjan que se calientan las manos. =
  Pretend to warm your hands.
*Toquen, canten, y luego adelántense
  al siguiente grupo.* = Play, sing,
  then move to the next group.

I Love the Mountains
(Amo las montañas)

Traditional Round
Spanish Version by MMH

Spanish: A - mo las mon - ta - ñas, A - mo las co - li - nas,
English: I____ love the moun - tains, I____ love the roll - ing hills,

A - mo las flo - res, A - mo los nar - ci - sos;
I love the flow - ers, I____ love the daf - fo - dils;

A - mo la ho - gue - ra cuan - do ba - ja la luz.
I____ love the fire - side when all the lights are low.

Bum - di - a - da, Bum - di - a - da, Bum - di - a - da, Bum - di - a - da.
Boom - dee - ah - da, Boom - dee - ah - da, Boom - dee - ah - da, Boom - dee - ah - da.

Macmillan/McGraw-Hill

DRY BONES
(Huesos)

Objective
Show simple musical form vocally and by
movement

Materials
Dry Bones (Huesos): Spanish **CD2:4**;
Pronunciation **CD2:5**; English **CD2:6**
Visual Aid M•29 (Worksheet): copy for each pair
Visual Aid M•30 (Song Map)

TEACHING THE LESSON

1. **Introduce the song.** Have students:
   - With a partner, follow the directions on **Visual Aid
     M•29** and complete the worksheet.
   - Name the body parts in English and Spanish, using
     Visual Aid M•30. Compare their work on **Visual
     Aid M•29** with **Visual Aid M•30.**
   - Play a game of "Simon Says," pointing to and
     naming the body parts with the Spanish names from
     Visual Aid M•30.

2. **Teach the song.** Have students:
   - Listen to "Dry Bones," following Visual Aid M•30.
   - Listen to and practice the pronunciation for the song.

- Practice saying the vocabulary words listed on the
  board. (See **Vocabulary,** below.)
- Following Visual Aid M•30, echo-sing the song as
  they touch each of the body parts they sing about.
- Compare the phrases of the B section and discuss
  the melodic direction of the song in relation to the
  order and location of the body parts named. (The
  melody moves up for each new phrase; the body
  parts are also named in ascending order.)

3. **Show form with movement/assess learning.**
   Have students:
   - Look at a display composed of three different items
     and discover the form ABC. (example: Draw a
     square, a triangle, and a circle on the board.)
   - Listen for and identify the three sections of the song.
   - Stand in a circle and sing the A section of the song
     while doing a pat-clap pattern; sing the B section,
     touching with the beat each body part named; and
     walk in a circle as they sing the C section.
   - Perform the song for each other in small groups.

RESOURCES

Extension
Have students find out how to name
the body parts in this song using a
third language. Perhaps someone in
the school knows German, French,
Korean, sign language, or other
languages.

Background
Although "Dry Bones" does not
appear among collected and studied
African American spirituals, the
lyrics have biblical sources. The
following is from Ezekiel, chapter 37:
"O dry bones, hear the word of the
Lord. Thus says the Lord God to
these bones: Behold, I will cause
breath to enter you, and you shall
live...and as I prophesied, there was
a noise, and behold, a rattling: and
the bones came together, bone to its
bone." The song's joyful rhythm and
its use of Ezekiel's prophetic words
communicate the traditional spiritual's
message of hope for a better life.

Vocabulary
hueso = bone
pie = foot
pierna = leg
rodilla = knee
cadera = hip
espalda = back
hombro = shoulder
cuello = neck
quijada = jaw
cabeza = head

Conversation Corner
Une los puntitos. = Connect the dots.
*Toquen la parte del cuerpo que diga
  la canción.* = Touch each body
  part as you sing about it.

Macmillan/McGraw-Hill

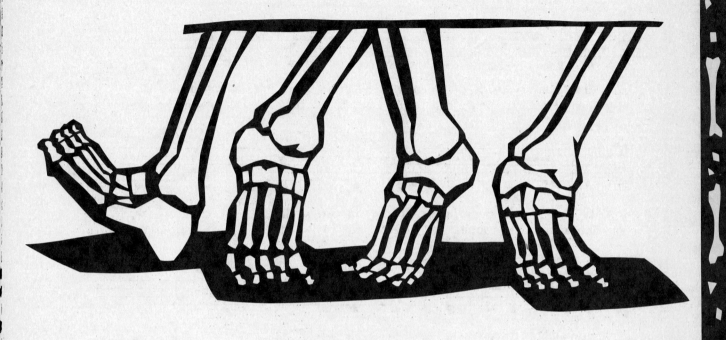

Dry Bones
(Huesos)

African American Spiritual
Spanish Version by MMH

Ⓐ Libre/Freely

C   G7   C

Spanish: E - ze-quiel gri - tó "¡Hue - sos!" E - ze-quiel gri - tó "¡Hue - sos!"
English: E - ze-kiel cried, "Them dry bones!" E - ze-kiel cried, "Them dry bones!"

C   G7   **1.** C

E - ze-quiel gri - tó "¡Hue - sos, y o - ye la pa - la - bra!" E -
E - ze-kiel cried, "Them dry bones, Now hear the Word of the Lord!" — E -

2. C   *accelerando*   **Ⓑ**

la - bra!"   El hue - so del pie con la pier - na,
Lord!" —   The foot — bone con - nect - ed to the leg bone,

Macmillan/McGraw-Hill

El hue - so de la pier - na con la ro - di - lla,
The leg____ bone con - nect - ed to the knee bone,

El hue - so de la ro - di - lla con la ca - de - ra,
The knee____ bone__ con - nect - ed to the hip - bone,

El hue - so de la ca - de - ra con la es - pal - da,
The hip - bone__ con - nect - ed to the back - bone,

El hue - so de la es - pal - da con el del hom - bro,
The back - bone__ con - nect - ed to__ the shoul - der bone,

El hue - so del hom - bro con el del cue - llo,
The shoul - der bone con - nect - ed to__ the neck bone,

El hue - so del cue - llo con la qui - ja - da,
The neck____ bone con - nect - ed to the jaw - bone,

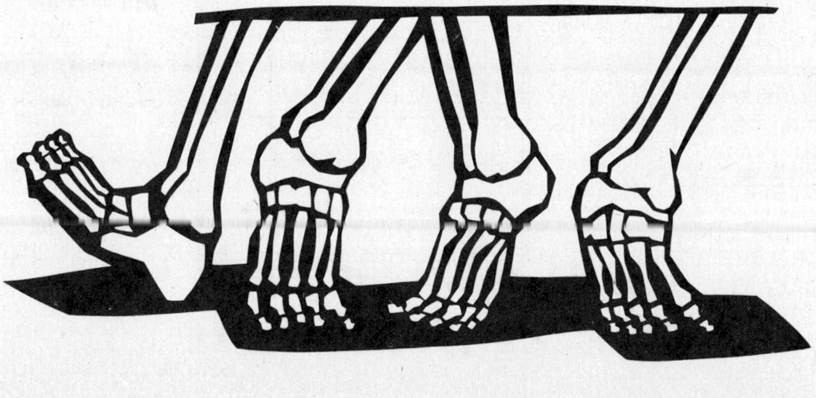

La qui - ja - da con la ca - be - za,
The__ jaw - bone con - nect - ed to the head bone,

Y o - ye la pa - la - bra.
Now hear the Word of the Lord.__

C *allegro*

E - sos hue - sos van a ca - mi - nar, e -
Them bones, them bones gon - na walk a - round, Them

sos hue - sos van a ca - mi - nar, e - sos hue - sos van a
bones, them bones gon - na walk a - round, Them bones, them bones gon - na

ca - mi - nar, y o - ye la pa - la - bra.
walk a - round, Now hear the Word of the Lord.__

Macmillan/McGraw-Hill

THE GHOST OF JOHN
(El fantasma de Juan)

Objective
Sing with appropriate body position and breathing

Materials
The Ghost of John (El fantasma de Juan): Spanish **CD2:7**; Pronunciation **CD2:8**; English **CD2:9**
Visual Aid M•31 (Song Map)
Visual Aid M•2 (Vocal Development): one for each pair; cover bottom section before copying

TEACHING THE LESSON

1. **Introduce the song.** Have students:
   - Listen to themselves as they make ghost sounds on *Oo* and decide if the sounds were smooth and connected or uneven and disconnected. (smooth and connected)

2. **Teach the song.** Have students:
   - Listen to "The Ghost of John" while following **Visual Aid M•31** and pay special attention to the singing on *Oo*.
   - Discuss whether the singing on *Oo* was smooth and connected or uneven and disconnected. (smooth and connected)
   - Discuss the meaning of the words.

   - Listen to and practice the pronunciation of the words while following Visual Aid M•31.
   - Practice saying the vocabulary words listed on the board. (See **Vocabulary,** below.)
   - Echo-sing, then sing the song.

3. **Teach the singing skills/assess learning.**
   Have students:
   - Look at the Body Position section of **Visual Aid M•2** and practice the position shown.
   - Work with partners as they practice the body position, giving feedback such as: "Back is straight, shoulders are relaxed, head is straight."
   - Use this body position while singing the song.
   - Look at the Breathing section of Visual Aid M•2. Practice slow, smooth breathing while their partners give feedback such as: "Your fingers are slowly moving apart as you inhale. They are moving slowly back together as you exhale." Switch roles.
   - With their bodies in singing position, breathe appropriately and sing the *Oo* phrase from the song.
   - Listen to the recording while following Visual Aid M•31. Take a full breath, then slowly release the air with a hissing sound through each phrase.
   - Sing the song using one full breath for each phrase.
   - Divide into two groups, one to sing and the other to listen. Listen for smooth and connected singing on *Oo* as each group demonstrates appropriate body position and breathing while singing the song.

RESOURCES

Creating Gestures
Have students in small groups make up smooth gestures to dramatize the pictures in the song map, then sing the song using the motions.

Vocal Ostinato
Have one group sing the following ostinato while another sings the song.

Playing Instruments
Have students add the following Orff accompaniment to the song.

Vocabulary
fantasma = ghost
huesos = bones
cutis = skin
frío = chilly

Conversation Corner
Mantengan su cuerpo así. = Hold your body like this.
Ensayen la respiración. = Practice breathing.
Ensayen con un compañero. = Work with a partner to practice these.

Macmillan/McGraw-Hill

The Ghost of John
(El fantasma de Juan)

English Words and Music
by Martha Grubb
Spanish Version by MMH

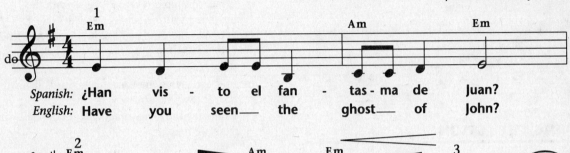

Spanish: ¿Han vis - to el fan - tas - ma de Juan?
English: Have you seen the ghost of John?

Hue - sos blan - cos sin cu - tis, Oo, oo,
Long white bones with the skin all gone, Oo, oo,

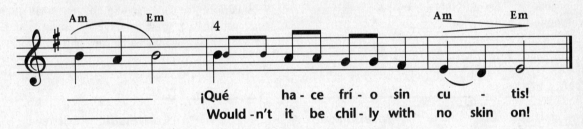

¡Qué ha - ce frí - o sin cu - tis!
Would -n't it be chil - ly with no skin on!

HAMBONE
(Paco)

Objective
Sing individually and in small groups

Materials
Hambone (Paco): Spanish **CD2:10**; Pronunciation **CD2:11**; English **CD2:12**
Visual Aid M•32 (Song Map)
Visual Aid M•33 (Worksheet): copy for each small group

TEACHING THE LESSON

1. Introduce the song. Have students:
- List a few items they would like to receive as gifts.
- Try to find a rhyming word for each item listed.

2. Teach the song. Have students:
- Listen as you tell them "Hambone" is a song about someone who gets gifts that don't work and gets new gifts to replace them.
- Perform a pat-clap pattern with the beat as they listen to the song.
- Discover that each verse relates to the previous verse. (example: Verse 2 begins with the mockingbird/*sinsonte* that ended Verse 1.)
- Listen to the song and follow **Visual Aid M•32**.
- Listen to and practice the pronunciation for the song.
- Practice saying the vocabulary words listed on the board. (See **Vocabulary,** below.)
- Echo-sing the song, practicing it with and without the song map.

3. Sing individually and in small groups/assess learning. Have students:
- Take turns being the leader as the class echo-sings each phrase of the song.
- Form small groups and create their own verses, following the directions on **Visual Aid M•33**.
- Perform the song again, a different small group leading each verse from the worksheet, and the rest of the class echo-singing each phrase.

RESOURCES

Playing Instruments
1. Have students add the following rhythm-stick accompaniment.

2. Have them play the above rhythm on spoons by putting two spoons back to back and tapping the spoons between the knee and palm.

Vocabulary
sinsonte = mockingbird
anillo = diamond ring
espejo = looking glass
chiva = goat
mundo = world
esposa = wife
arroz = rice

Conversation Corner
¿Hay alguna palabra que se repita en el siguiente verso? = Are there any words that come back in the next verse?
¿Cuál es el orden de los regalos en la canción? = What is the order of the gifts in the song?

Macmillan/McGraw-Hill

Hambone

(Paco)

African American Hand Jive Game
Spanish Version by MMH

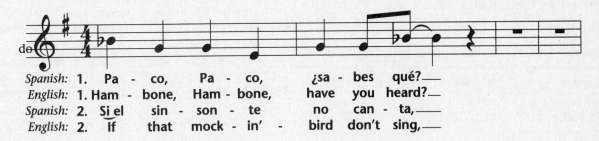

Spanish: 1. Pa - co, Pa - co, ¿sa - bes qué?___
English: 1. Ham - bone, Ham - bone, have you heard?___
Spanish: 2. Si el sin - son - te no can - ta,___
English: 2. If that mock - in' - bird don't sing,___

Pa - pi va a com-prar - me un sin - son - te.___
Pop - pa's gon - na buy me a mock - in' - bird.___
Pa - pi va a com-prar - me un a - ni - llo.___
Pop - pa's gon - na buy me a dia - mond ring.___

3. Si el anillo no me va,
   Papi va a comprarme un espejo.

3. If that diamond ring turns brass,
   Poppa's gonna buy me a looking glass.

4. Si el espejo se quiebra,
   Papi va a comprarme una chiva.

4. If that looking glass gets broke,
   Poppa's gonna buy me a billy goat.

5. Paco, Paco, ¿dónde has ido?
   Por el mundo y ya volví.

5. Hambone, Hambone, where you been?
   "Round the world and back again."

6. Paco, Paco, ¿y tu esposa?
   En la cocina comiendo arroz.

6. Hambone, Hambone, where's your wife?
   "She's in the kitchen eatin' rice."

DOWN THE RIVER
(Por el río)

Objective
Identify and use the musical symbols ♩, ♪, ♫♫, ♩.

Materials
Down the River (Por el río): Spanish **CD2:13**;
   Pronunciation **CD2:14**; English **CD2:15**;
   Performance Mix **CD2:16**
Visual Aid M•34 (Song Map)
Visual Aid M•35 (Notation): prepare as
   transparency (optional)

TEACHING THE LESSON

1. **Introduce the song.** Have students:
    *   Name bodies of water in English and Spanish.
        (lakes = *lagos;* rivers = *ríos;* oceans = *mares;*
        streams = *arroyos;* creeks = *ensenadas)*
    *   Describe each body named by how fast the water
        moves, types of fish in it, and how one might travel
        across it.

2. **Teach the song.** Have students:
    *   Listen to "Down the River," following **Visual Aid
        M•34.**

*   Discuss the meaning of the words.
*   Listen to and practice the pronunciation of the
    words while following the song map.
*   Practice saying the vocabulary words listed on the
    board. (See **Vocabulary,** below.)
*   Echo-sing each verse, then sing the entire song.

3. **Teach the rhythm notation/assess learning.**
    Have students:
    *   Look at **Visual Aid M•35** and practice clapping the
        rhythms as follows:
        For the dotted quarter note (♩.), hold one hand
        still and use the other hand to clap for one beat
        and slide for two beats.
        For the quarter note (♩), clap-slide, and for the
        eighth note (♪), clap once.
        Clap three times for the three beamed eighth
        notes (♫♫).
    *   Look at the refrain of "Down the River" and locate
        the rhythms, then clap the rhythm of the refrain at a
        slow tempo, using the motions practiced for each
        symbol.
    *   Clap the refrain again, as slowly as necessary,
        singing at the same time.

RESOURCES

Playing Instruments
Have students play the rhythm on
unpitched instruments as they sing.

Movement
  Formation: longways set of four or
five couples
  Verse: Head couple joins both
hands, sashays down the set (seven
slides, one side-skip) for eight beats,
and sashays back for eight beats.
  Refrain: Head couple reels down to
the foot of the set and stays. On the
next verse, the dance begins with a
new head couple. (A reel is a right-
hand swing with the partner, followed
by a left-hand swing with the next
person in the opposite line.)

Vocabulary
río = river
viento = wind
orilla = shore

Conversation Corner
¿Cómo cruza la gente el río? = How
   do people travel across a river?
Den palmadas así. = Clap this way.
*Toquen estos ritmos con un
   instrumento.* = Play an instrument
   on these rhythms.

Macmillan/McGraw-Hill

Down the River
(Por el río)

American River Chantey
Spanish Version by MMH

Estrofa/Verse

Spanish: 1.-2. El rí - o es - tá al - to y el ca - nal pro - fun - do, el
English: 1.-2. The riv - er is up and the chan - nel is deep, —— The

vien - to sí es - tá fuer - te.
wind is stead - y and strong. ——

(1.) Ay, qué a - le - gre
(1.) Oh, won't we have a
(2.) Ay, Dia - na, Dia - na,
(2.) Oh, Di - nah, put the

tiem - po te - ne - mos cuan - do na - ve - ga - mos.
jol - ly good time, As we go sail - ing a - long. ——
co - se la tor - ta
hoe - cake on, As

DOWN THE RIVER   (Por el río)   PAGE 2

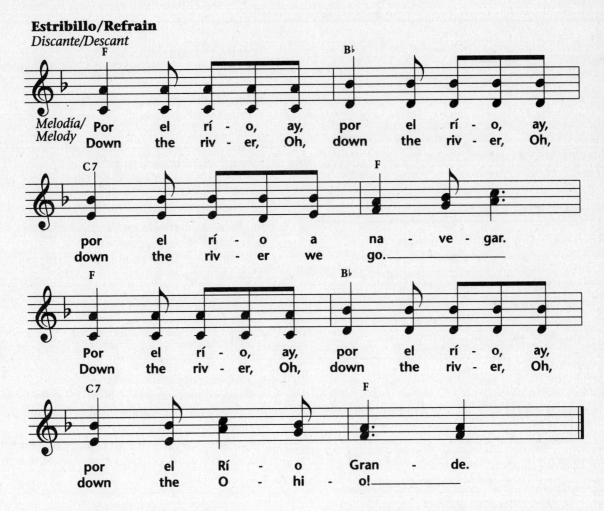

Estribillo/Refrain

Discante/Descant

Melodía/Melody

Por   el   rí - o,   ay,   por   el   rí - o,   ay,
Down   the   riv - er,   Oh,   down   the   riv - er,   Oh,

por   el   rí - o   a   na - ve - gar.
down   the   riv - er   we   go._____

Por   el   rí - o,   ay,   por   el   rí - o,   ay,
Down   the   riv - er,   Oh,   down   the   riv - er,   Oh,

por   el   Rí - o   Gran - de.
down   the   O - hi - o!_____

3. El río está alto y el canal profundo,
   el viento sí está fuerte.
   Golpea el agua en las orillas
   cuando navegamos.
   Estribillo

3. The river is up and the channel is deep,
   The wind is steady and strong.
   The waves do splash from shore to shore,
   As we go sailing along.
   Refrain

SWEET POTATOES
(Camotes dulces)

Objective
Perform and create ostinato accompaniments

Materials
Sweet Potatoes (Camotes dulces): Spanish
   CD2:17; Pronunciation **CD2:18**; English **CD2:19**
Visual Aid M•36 (Flashcards): one set
Visual Aid M•37 (Song Map)

TEACHING THE LESSON

1. **Introduce the song.** Have students:
    *   Form three groups. Perform a spoken canon called "Comida favorita" (Favorite Food) using the first three rhythms from **Visual Aid M•36**. Group 1 starts the canon, and each new group enters after the preceding group has performed its rhythm twice. Each group says its rhythm 12 times.

2. **Teach the song.** Have students:
    *   Listen to "Sweet Potatoes" and follow **Visual Aid M•37**.
    *   Discuss the meaning of the words.
    *   Listen to and practice the pronunciation for the song.
    *   Practice saying the vocabulary words listed on the board. (See **Vocabulary,** below.)
    *   Echo-sing, then sing the song, following the song map.

3. **Perform and create ostinatos/assess learning.** Have students:
    *   Listen as you define an ostinato as a repeated pattern that accompanies a song.
    *   Practice the following vocal ostinato using Pattern 4 from Visual Aid M•36.

    *   Sing the song with the ostinato.
    *   Create ostinatos in small groups, using the name of a favorite food, a restaurant, "yum-yum" sounds, and so on.
    *   Perform the song with each of the ostinatos created.

RESOURCES

Notation
Have students notate their ostinatos, using Parts 5 or 6 of Visual Aid M•36.

Vocabulary
camotes dulces = sweet potatoes
cenados = having eaten supper
almohada = pillow
duérmanse ya = go to sleep quickly
nos lavamos la cara = wash our faces

Conversation Corner
Repite la frase muchas veces. =
   Repeat the phrase over and over.
Vamos a crear nuestro propio ostinato. = Let's create our own ostinato.

Sweet Potatoes
(Camotes dulces)

Louisiana Creole Folk Song
Spanish Version by MMH

Spanish: **1.** Co - ci - na - mos ca - mo - tes dul - ces,
English: **1.** Soon as we all___ cook sweet po - ta - toes,
Spanish: **2.** Ya ce - na - dos___ Ma - mi nos lla - ma,
English: **2.** Soon as sup - per's___ gone, Mam - ma calls us,

Los ca - mo - tes, los ca - mo - tes.
sweet po - ta - toes, sweet po - ta - toes.
Ma - mi lla - ma, Ma - mi lla - ma.
Mam - ma calls us, Mam - ma calls us.

Co - ci - na - mos ca - mo - tes dul - ces,
Soon as we all___ cook sweet po - ta - toes,
Ya ce - na - dos___ Ma - mi nos lla - ma,
Soon as sup - per's___ gone, Mam - ma calls us,

Co - men - se - los ya.
Eat 'em while they're hot.
Váy - an - se a - cos - tar.
Get a - long to bed.

3. Con la cabeza en la almohada,
   Almohada, almohada.
   Con la cabeza en la almohada,
   Duérmanse ya.

4. Tan pronto que canta el gallo,
   Al amanecer, al amanecer.
   Tan pronto que canta el gallo,
   Nos lavamos la cara.

3. Soon's we touch our heads to the pillow,
   To the pillow, to the pillow.
   Soon's we touch our heads to the pillow,
   Go to sleep right smart!

4. Soon's the rooster crow in the morning,
   In the morning, in the morning.
   Soon's the rooster crow in the morning,
   Gotta wash our face.

TAKE TIME IN LIFE
(Vive la vida)

Objective
Sing short sections of a song in small groups

Materials
Take Time in Life (Vive la vida): Spanish **CD2:20**;
  Pronunciation **CD2:21**; English **CD2:22**
Visual Aid M•38 (Cue Cards): one set
Visual Aid M•39 (Song Map)

TEACHING THE LESSON

1. **Introduce the song.** Have students:
   - Play charades by acting out something they do to relax, using **Visual Aid M•38** for ideas.
   - List on the board things that their family and friends always seem to be rushing to get done.

2. **Teach the song.** Have students:
   - Listen to "Take Time in Life," following **Visual Aid M•39**.
   - Discuss the meaning of the words. (Advice: don't rush through life without enjoying it.)

   - Compare any words in the song that might relate to their lists on the board.
   - Listen to and practice the pronunciation of the words while following the song map.
   - Practice saying the vocabulary words listed on the board. (See **Vocabulary,** below.)
   - Echo-sing one verse at a time, then sing the entire song.

3. **Introduce the singing activity/assess learning.** Have students:
   - Follow Visual Aid M•39 as you sing the song. Locate lines in the song that could be sung by a small group. (first two lines of each verse)
   - Follow the song map again, singing the small group part and listening when you sing the last two lines.
   - Work in groups of three, each group selecting and practicing one of the verses, then performing it for the class, with the rest of the groups joining on the last two lines. Continue until all small groups have performed.

RESOURCES

Playing Chords
Have students accompany the song on autoharp by following the chords written above the notation.

Singing Solos
Select students to sing individual lines of the song. Have the class speak the words below as an interlude to provide time for the soloists to choose other singers to take their place.

Movement
Formation: double circle, partners standing shoulder to shoulder; inside circle facing clockwise, outside circle facing counterclockwise

Measures 1-4: Both circles walk forward four steps, stand still while clapping four beats, walk backward four steps, clap four beats.

Measures 5-8: Face partner, high five on each *take time in life,* alternating right and left hands. On *far way to go,* both partners take one side step to the left to be in front of a new partner, then turn to the original direction they were facing and repeat.

Vocabulary
hermano = brother
vida = life
gente = people
tío = uncle
hijo = son
joven = young man

Conversation Corner
Adivinen lo que estoy haciendo. = Guess what I'm doing.
Canten con este grupo. = Sing with this group.

Take Time in Life

(Vive la vida)

Liberian Folk Song
Spanish Version by MMH

3. Iba caminando, la gente me habló,
   dijeron vive la vida,
     vive la vida.
   Joven, vive la vida, Joven,
     vive la vida,
   Joven, vive la vida
     porque es largo el camino.

3. I was passing by, Some people called me in,
   And they said to me, My young man,
     take time in life.
   Young man, take time in life, Young man,
     take time in life,
   Young man, take time in life
     'cause you got far way to go.

THE TWELVE DAYS OF CHRISTMAS
(Los doce días de Navidad)

Objective
Sing in small groups

Materials
The Twelve Days of Christmas (Los doce días de Navidad): Spanish **CD2:23**; Pronunciation **CD2:24**; English **CD2:25**
Visual Aid M•40 (Counting Chart)
Visual Aid M•41 (Worksheet)
Visual Aid M•42 (Song Map): one copy, or transparency (optional), cut into twelve strips

TEACHING THE LESSON

1. **Introduce the song.** Have students:
    *   Count from *first* to *twelfth* in English and in Spanish, using **Visual Aid M•40.**
    *   List twelve things they would like to get as gifts, using **Visual Aid M•41.**

2. **Teach the song.** Have students:
    *   Listen to "The Twelve Days of Christmas," following **Visual Aid M•42.**

*   Compare their lists on Visual Aid M•41 to the gifts named in the song. Discuss where and how the person who received all those gifts might have lived, by using the information in the song. (might have lived in a place with a barn, bird cages, a pond or lake; may have had cows to milk; and so on) Decide how the source of the song (England) and the time it was written (long ago) determined the gifts to be included. Use the complete Visual Aid M•41 to discuss how they might change the song for today's society.
*   Listen to and practice the pronunciation for the song.
*   Practice saying the vocabulary words listed on the board. (See **Vocabulary,** below.)
*   Echo-sing, then sing the song, following Visual Aid M•42.

3. **Assign small singing groups/assess learning.** Have students:
    *   Form 12 groups, each to learn an assigned verse by using a verse strip from a copy of Visual Aid M•42 that has been cut into 12 strips.
    *   Perform the song, each group singing its assigned verse at the appropriate time and placing its verse strip on the overhead projector.
    *   Take turns singing different verses.

RESOURCES

Creating New Verses
1. Let students use their work on Visual Aid M•41 to compose their own song, for example, "The Twelve Days of My Birthday."
2. Have them create new verses about gifts from 12 different countries.

Vocabulary
Navidad = Christmas
perdiz = partridge
peral = pear tree
palomitas = doves
gallinitas = hens
gorriones = sparrows
anillos = rings
gansos = geese
cisnes = swans
lecheras = milkers
tamborileros = drummers
flautistas = pipers
bailarinas = dancers
saltadores = jumpers

Conversation Corner
¿Qué regalos te gustaría recibir? = What gifts would you like to get?
Nombra los regalos en la misma orden que ocurren en la canción. = Name the gifts in the song in order.
Aprende con tu compañero(a) el verso que está en el papel. = Work with your partner to learn the verse on the paper I give you.
Canta tu verso cuando lleguemos a tu número en la canción. = Sing your verse when we get to your number in the song.

The Twelve Days of Christmas
(Los doce días de Navidad)

English Carol
Spanish Version by MMH

Spanish: 1. En el pri - mer dí - a des - pués de Na - vi - dad, re - ci -
English: 1. On the first day of Christ - mas my true love sent to me:____ A

bí u - na per - diz en un pe - ral. 2. En el se - gun - do dí - a des -
par - tridge___ in a pear tree. 2. On the sec - ond day of Christ - mas my

pués de Na - vi - dad, re - ci - bí dos pa - lo - mi - tas y u - na per - diz en un pe - ral.
true love sent to me: Two___ tur - tle doves,_ and_ a par - tridge_ in a pear tree.

THE TWELVE DAYS OF CHRISTMAS   (Los doce días de Navidad)   PAGE 2

3. En el ter - cer dí - a des - pués de Na - vi - dad, re - ci -
3. On the third day of Christ - mas my true love sent to me:

bí tres ga lli ni tas, dos pa lo mi tas, y u na per-diz en un pe
Three French hens, two tur-tle doves, and a par-tridge in a pear

ral. 4. En el cuar - to dí - a des - pués de Na - vi - dad, re - ci -
tree. 4. On the fourth day of Christ-mas my true love sent to me:

bí cua-tro go - rrio - nes, dos pa - lo - mi-tas, y u-na per-diz en un pe
Four col - ly birds, two tur-tle doves, and a par-tridge in a pear
tres ga - lli - ni - tas,
three French hens,

ral. 5. En el quin - to dí - a des - pués de Na - vi - dad, re - ci -
tree. 5. On the fifth day of Christ - mas my true love sent to me:

Macmillan/McGraw-Hill

Música para todos for Intermediate Grades

5. bí cin - co a - ni - llos de o - ro,   cua - tro go - rrio - nes, tres ga - lli - ni - tas,
6.-12. cin - co a - ni - llos de o - ro,
5.-12. Five_____ gold - en _ rings, _   four_ col - ly birds, _ three French _ hens, _

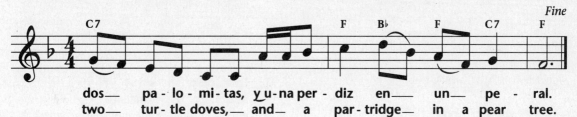

dos_____ pa - lo - mi - tas, y u - na per - diz en_____ un_____ pe - ral.
two_____ tur - tle doves, _ and_ a par - tridge_ in a pear tree.

6.-12. En el sex - to dí - a des - pués de Na - vi - dad, re - ci -
6.-12. On the sixth day of Christ - mas my true love sent to me:

6. bí seis lin - dos gan - sos,
6. Six_____ geese a - lay - ing,

7. séptimo . . . siete cisnes,	7. seventh . . . Seven swans a-swimming,
8. octavo . . . ocho lecheras,	8. eighth . . . Eight maids a-milking,
9. noveno . . . nueve tamborileros,	9. ninth . . . Nine drummers drumming,
10. décimo . . . diez flautistas,	10. tenth . . . Ten pipers piping,
11. undécimo . . . once bailarinas,	11. eleventh . . . Eleven ladies dancing,
12. duodécimo . . . doce saltadores,	12. twelfth . . . Twelve lords a-leaping,

AULD LANG SYNE
(El calor de la amistad)

Objective
Sing in small groups

Materials
Auld Lang Syne (El calor de la amistad): Spanish
CD2:26; Pronunciation **CD2:27**; English
CD2:28
Visual Aid M•43 (Illustration): prepare as
transparency (optional)
Visual Aid M•44 (Song Map)
Visual Aid M•45 (Cue Cards): one set

TEACHING THE LESSON

1. **Introduce the song.** Have students:
    *   Look at **Visual Aid M•43** and discuss what time of
        year it is and how they know. (New Year's Eve —
        because of smiles, party hats, clock showing 12
        midnight, moon showing through the window, party
        clothes)
    *   Discuss the purpose of celebrating New Year's Eve.
        (say goodbye to the past year, welcome in the New
        Year, remember old friends, make new friends)
    *   Name ways people celebrate New Year's Eve.
        (parties, dances, dinners, Times Square ball falling
        at midnight)

2. **Teach the song.** Have students:
    *   Listen to "Auld Lang Syne," following **Visual Aid
        M•44**.
    *   Discuss the meaning of the words. (remembering
        friends)
    *   Listen to and practice the pronunciation of the
        words while following the song map.
    *   Practice saying the vocabulary words listed on the
        board. (See **Vocabulary,** below.)
    *   Echo-sing each verse, then sing the entire song.

3. **Introduce the small group singing/assess
    learning.** Have students:
    *   Form groups of three or four members.
    *   Pretend they are at a New Year's Eve party at
        midnight.
    *   Within each group, select and practice a verse to
        sing when it is their group's time to leave the party.
        Practice a dramatization of the scene.
    *   Draw a card made from **Visual Aid M•45** for each
        group and use the times shown to determine the
        order in which the groups sing their chosen verses
        and perform their dramatizations.
    *   Sing the song as a class, being sure to use one full
        breath for each phrase.
    *   In the groups, perform the dramatizations and
        verses in the correct order and pretend to leave the
        party after their group's performance. Sing the
        refrain as a class each time it occurs.

RESOURCES

Singing Solos
Have students take turns singing a
verse as soloist. All students join in
on the refrain.

Playing Instruments
Have students play the chord roots
of the song on bass/tenor pitched
instruments. Have them form two
groups, one singing the melody and
the other playing the chord roots.

Vocabulary
tacita = cup
bondad = kindness

Conversation Corner
¿Cómo celebra la gente el año nuevo?
= How do people celebrate the
New Year?
Inventen movimientos para este verso. =
Make up movements to this verse.
Enseñen a la clase. = Show the class.

Macmillan/McGraw-Hill

Auld Lang Syne
(El calor de la amistad)

Scotch Air
English Words by Robert Burns
Spanish Version by MMH

Estrofa/Verse

Spanish: 1. ¿Ol - vi - da - rás nues - tra a - mis - tad y el
English: 1. Should auld ac - quain - tance— be for - got, And
Spanish: 2. To - ma mi ma - no a - mi - go y
English: 2. And here's a hand, my— trust - y frien', And

tiem - po pa - sa - do? ¿Ol - vi - da - rás nues - tra
nev - er brought to mind? Should auld ac - quain - tance—
tú me la da - rás u - na ta - ci - ta—
gie's a hand o' thine; We'll tak' a cup o'—

a - mis - tad y el tiem - po pa - sa - do?
be for - got, And days of auld lang syne?
de bon - dad por nues - tra a - mis - tad.
kind - ness yet, For auld— lang— syne.

Estribillo/Refrain

A - diós, a - diós, a - mi - go fiel, Muy pron - to he de par - tir,
For auld— lang— syne, my dear, For auld— lang— syne;

pe - ro a - quí siem - pre que - da - rá el ca - lor de la a - mis - tad.
We'll tak' a cup o' kind - ness yet, For— auld— lang— syne.

La cumbia

Ai - e · tim - ba - le - ro,

bai - le   cum - bia

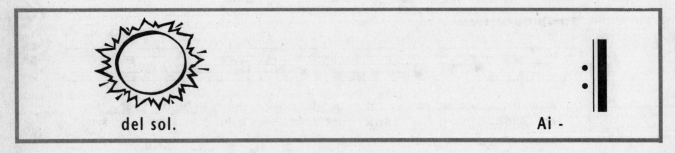

del sol.   Ai -

Name _____

Singing Correctly
(Para cantar bien)

Body Position
Posición del cuerpo

straight back
espalda recta

Breathing
Respiración

hands on midsection
manos en la parte abdominal del cuerpo

inhale
inspiren

slowly exhale
espiren despacito

Vowels
Vocales

Ai   e   i   a   e —   o,

ai   e   u   ia   e   o.

Macmillan/McGraw-Hill

Name _____

La cumbia

Aie   tim - ba - le - ro.

Aie   tim -

ba - le - ro.

Don Martín

ti-ri-rin-tin-tín,

Su chiquitín,

De sarampión

to- ro-ron-ton-tón.

to-ro-ron-ton-tón,

Se le murió

ti-ri-rin-tin-tín,

A Don Martín,

Oh, Don Martín,
ti-ri-rin-tin-tín,
His children cried,
to-ro-ron-ton-tón,
They got the measles,
ti-ri-rin-tin-tín,
And then they died!
to-ro-ron-ton-tón.

Música para todos for Intermediate Grades

Macmillan/McGraw-Hill

Name _____

Entren santos peregrinos
(Enter, Holy Pilgrims)

Entren   **santos peregrinos,**   **peregrinos,**
Enter in,   all holy pilgrims,   holy pilgrims.

Reciban este rincón,   **que aunque es pobre la morada,**   **la morada,**
Welcome to our humble grove.   There is little we can give you,   we can give you,

Os la doy de corazón.
Still we welcome you with love.

Entren santos peregrinos
(Enter, Holy Pilgrims)

D   G   A

En-tren san-tos pe-re-gri-nos, pe-re-gri-nos,＿ Re - ci -
En - ter in,   all ho-ly pil-grims, ho-ly pil-grims. Wel-come

ban es - te   rin - cón, que aun-que es po - bre   la   mo -
to   our hum - ble grove. There   is   lit - tle we   can

ra - da, la   mo - ra-da,＿ Os la doy de   co - ra - zón.
give you, we can give you, Still we wel-come you with love.

Name _____

Entren santos peregrinos

(Enter, Holy Pilgrims)

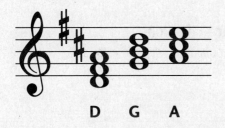

D G A

D E F♯ G A B C♯ D

En - tren san - tos pe - re - gri - nos, pe - re - gri - nos, ___ Re - ci -
En - ter in,   all ho - ly pil - grims, ho - ly pil - grims. Wel - come

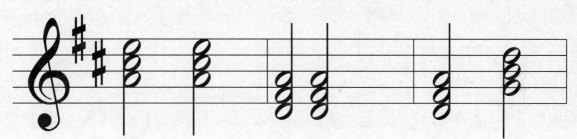

ban es - te   rin - cón, que aun - que es   po - bre   la   mo -
to   our hum - ble grove. There   is   lit - tle   we can

ra - da, la   mo - ra - da, ___ Os la doy de   co - ra - zón.
give you, we can give you, Still we wel - come you with love.

With Others or Alone

(Acompañado o solo)

Things I do with family and friends:
Cosas que hago con mi familia o amigos:

1. _____

2. _____

3. _____

4. _____

5. _____

Things I do alone:
Cosas que hago cuando estoy solo:

1. _____

2. _____

3. _____

4. _____

5. _____

Música para todos **for Intermediate Grades**

Name _____

De allacito carnavalito

(The Carnival Is Coming)

Carnavalito

De allacito, de allacito,
Ev'ryone there is coming

ya viene el carnavalito;
down to the carnavalito.

Todos bajan en pareja,
Ev'ryone comes down in couples,

yo voy bajando solito.
I am a lonely solo.

VISUAL AIDS   M•11   Cue Cards

Choose a Movement
(Elijan un movimiento)

twirl
giren

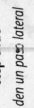

step-side
den un paso lateral

hop on one foot
brinquen sobre un pie

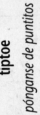

tiptoe
pónganse de puntitos

walk backwards
caminen hacia atrás

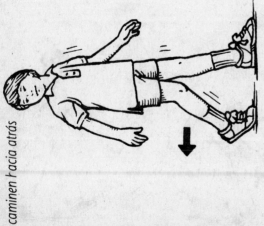

move like an animal
muévense como un animal

Música para todos for Intermediate Grades

Name _____

Traveling to a Nearby Town
(Viajando a un pueblo cercano)

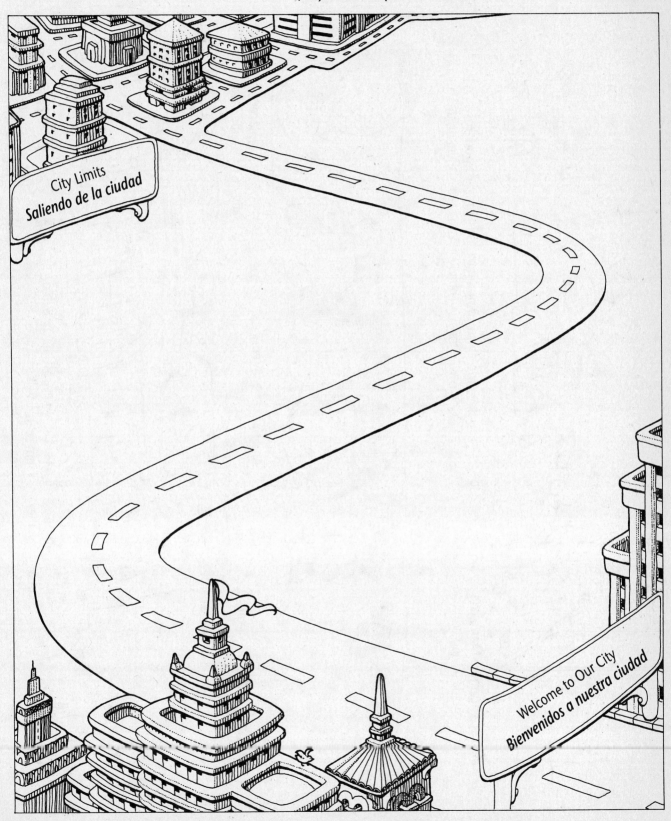

City Limits
Saliendo de la ciudad

Welcome to Our City
Bienvenidos a nuestra ciudad

Name _____

VISUAL AIDS   M•13   Song Map

Alegría, alegría
(Joy, Joy)

Hacia Belén se encamina María con su amante esposo
On to *Belén* goes Maria, loving husband close beside her.

llevando en su compañía a todo en Dios poderoso.
God is with them, a companion, to protect them on their journey.

Alegría   Alegría,   Alegría,   Alegría   y   placer
Alegría   *Alegría*   *Alegría,*   *Alegría*   and   pleasure today.
                                                  joy

que la Virgen va de paso con su esposo hacia Belén.
On to *Belén*, they will journey, they will pass us on their way.

BELÉN

Macmillan/McGraw-Hill

Name _____

Musical Symbols
(Símbolos musicales)

staff
pentagrama

treble clef
clave de sol

key signature
armadura

meter signature
signatura de compás

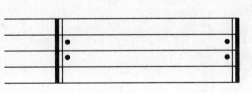

repeat signs
repeticiones

first ending
coda primera

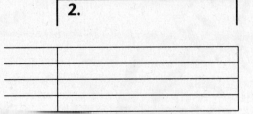

second ending
coda segunda

double bar line
barra doble

Macmillan/McGraw-Hill

Chíu, chíu, chíu

Chíu, chíu, chíu, chíu,
chíu, chíu, chíu, chíu.
Canta, canta paja'ito.
Que tu cantar me alegra el corazón.

*Chíu, chíu, chíu, chíu,
chíu, chíu, chíu, chíu.
Canta, canta pajarito.
Your merry singing sets my heart aglow.*

Con tus gorjeos,   You merry chirping;
con tu trinar,   you roundelay,
Despierta el alba,   You bring the dawning,
la noche ya se va.   the shadows fade away.

Canta, canta, pajarito.
Canta, canta tu canción,
Mira que la vida es triste
y tu cantar me alegra el corazón.

*Canta, canta pajarito.
Sing the songs that cheer me so.
See, my life is full of sorrow,
your merry singing sets my heart aglow.*

Macmillan/McGraw-Hill

Bird Songs
(Sonidos de las aves)

pollito

pío, pío

peep peep

chick

gallo

qui qui ri quí

cock-a-doodle-doo

rooster

tecolote

hoo-hoo   *hoo-hoo*

owl

paloma

cucurrú

coo coo

dove

Macmillan/McGraw-Hill

Name _____

El quelite
(The Village)

rooster
gallito

Exit

Al pie de un verde quelite
me dio sueño y me dormí,
y me despertó un gallito
cantando "qui qui ri quí."
Yo no canto porque sí puedo,
ni porque mi voz sea buena,
canto porque tengo gusto
en mi tierra y en la ajena.
Mañana, me voy mañana,
mañana me voy de aquí,
y el consuelo que me queda
que se han de acordar de mi.

At the edge of a green *quelite*,
I stopped awhile there to sleep.
A rooster cried out and woke me.
He sang a "qui qui ri quí."
I don't sing because I'm able,
nor because my voice is good.
I sing because I feel joy
in my land and foreign lands.
Tomorrow I will be leaving,
and who can tell where I'll be?
But here is my consolation:
that someone remembers me.

Name _____

El quelite
(The Village)

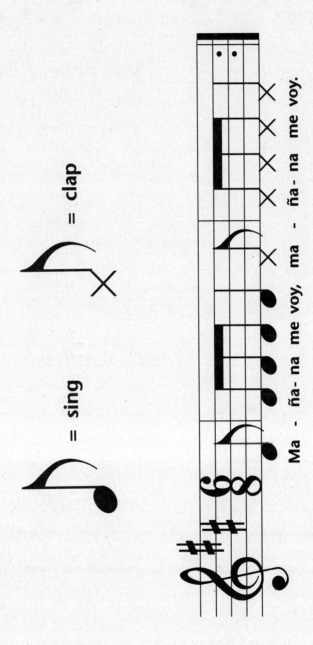

Name _____

Make a Menu
(Preparando un menú)

Music Cafe
M E N U

Appetizers/_Primeros platos_

_____ $ _____

_____ $ _____

_____ $ _____

Soups & Salads/_Caldos y Ensaladas_

_____ $ _____

_____ $ _____

_____ $ _____

Main Dishes/_Platos principales_

_____ $ _____

_____ $ _____

_____ $ _____

_____ $ _____

_____ $ _____

Desserts/_Postres_

_____ $ _____

_____ $ _____

Beverages/_Bebidas_

_____ $ _____

_____ $ _____

Name _____

Si me dan pasteles
(When You Bring *Pasteles*)

Si me dan

When you bring _____

dénmelos

Give me only _____

que pasteles

People who eat _____

empachan a la

all have _____

Si me dan

If you give me _____

no me den

don't give me _____

que   **me dijo**

My _____ has told me

que se lo llevara.

"Bring them straight home to me!"

Interludio/Interlude:
Le lo lai, le lo lai.
Le lo lai, le lo lai.

Name _____

Words to Learn
(Palabras para aprender)

pasteles

· · · · · · · · · · · · · ·

holiday patties of meat
and plantain

fríos

· · · · · · · · · · · · ·

cold ones

calientes

· · · · · · · · · · ·

hot ones

gente

· · · · · · · · · · · · ·

people

cuchara

· · · · · · · · · · ·

spoon

arroz

· · · · · · · · · · ·

rice

mamá

· · · · · · · · · · ·

mom, mother

Campanas vespertinas
(Evening Bells)

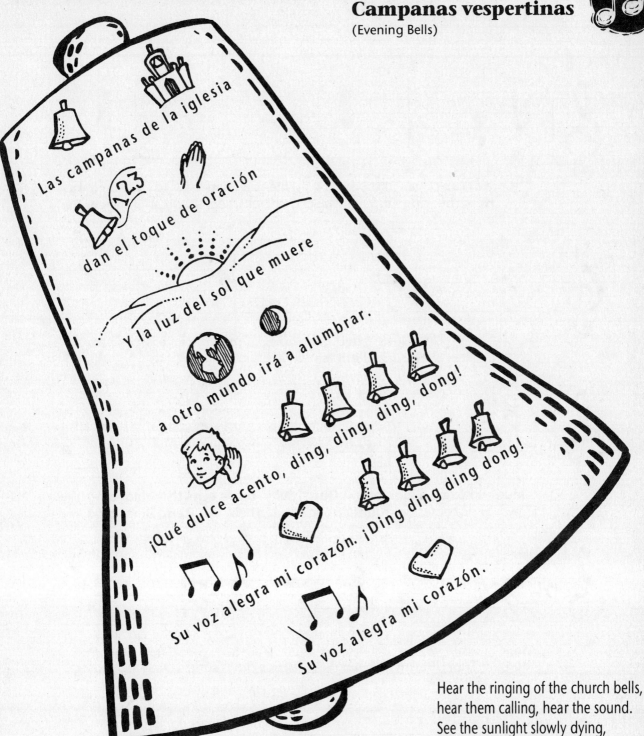

Las campanas de la iglesia

dan el toque de oración

Y la luz del sol que muere

a otro mundo irá a alumbrar.

¡Qué dulce acento, ding, ding, ding, dong!

Su voz alegra mi corazón. ¡Ding ding ding dong!

Su voz alegra mi corazón.

Hear the ringing of the church bells,
hear them calling, hear the sound.
See the sunlight slowly dying,
as the evening comes around.
How sweet their accent,
Ding, ding, ding, dong!
They lift my heart with their evensong.
Ding ding ding dong!
They lift my heart with their evensong.

Campanas vespertinas
(Evening Bells)

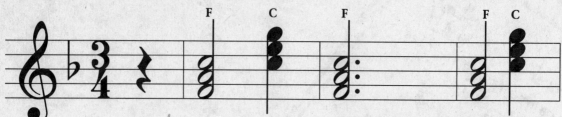

Las cam - pa - nas de la i - gle - sia dan el to - que de o - ra-
Hear the ring - ing of the church bells, hear them call-ing, hear the

ción. Y la luz del sol que mue - re a o - tro
sound. See the sun - light slow - ly dy - ing, as the

mun - do i - rá a a - lum - brar. ¡Qué dul - ce a - cen - to, ding, ding, ding,
eve - ning comes a - round. How sweet their ac-cent, Ding, ding, ding,

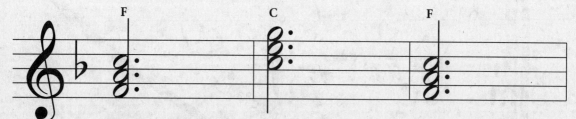

dong! Su voz a - le - gra mi co - ra - zón. ¡Ding ding ding
dong! They lift my heart with their e - ven - song. Ding ding ding

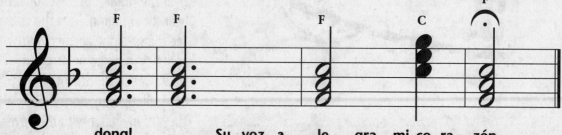

dong! Su voz a - le - gra mi co - ra - zón.
dong! They lift my heart With their e - ven - song.

Macmillan/McGraw-Hill

Name _____

De colores
(Many Colors)

De colores, de colores se visten los campos en la primavera.
Oh, the colors! Oh, the colors we see in the blossoming fields in the springtime.

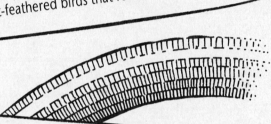

De colores, de colores son los pajarillos que vienen de afuera.
All the colors, all the colors of bright-feathered birds that return from a distance.

De colores, de colores es el arco iris que vemos lucir.
Oh, the colors! Oh, the colors that light up the sky in a beautiful rainbow!

Y por eso los grandes amores de muchos colores me gustan a mí.
And the colors of true love are brightest, and these are the colors I love most of all.

Y por eso los grandes amores de muchos colores me gustan a mí.
And the colors of true love are brightest, and these are the colors I love most of all.

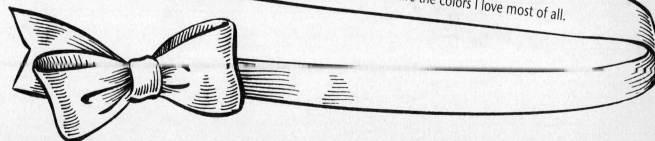

Macmillan/McGraw-Hill

Música para todos for Intermediate Grades

81

Name _____

Name the Colors
(A nombrar colores)

red

rojo

green

verde

white

blanco

blue

azul

black

negro

_____

_____

Música para todos for Intermediate Grades

Macmillan/McGraw-Hill

Name _____

Name the Colors
(A nombrar colores)

orange

anaranjado

pink

rosa

brown

café

yellow

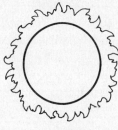

amarillo

purple

morado

_____

_____

Name _____

Giving Thanks
(Damos gracias)

For Thy Gracious Blessings
Por sus bendiciones

1

* Por sus bendiciones,
For Thy gracious blessings,

2

For Thy wondrous Word, For Thy loving kindness, We give thanks, Oh Lord.

* * Le damos gracias.

Por su caridad, Por su buena voluntad,

For Health and Strength
Salud y fuerza

* Salud y fuerza,
For health and strength and daily food

1

* Dios.
Oh, Lord.

We praise Thy name,

gracias

2

alimento: Damos

84

Macmillan/McGraw-Hill

Name _____

I Love the Mountains
(Amo las montañas)

Amo las montañas,
I love the mountains,

Amo las colinas,
I love the rolling hills,

Amo las flores,
I love the flowers,

Amo los narcisos;
I love the daffodils;

Amo la hoguera
I love the fireside

cuando baja la luz.
when all the lights are low.

 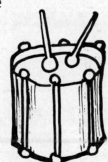  

Bum-di-a-da,   **Bum-di-a-da,**   **Bum-di-a-da,**   **Bum-di-a-da.**
Boom-dee-ah-da,   Boom-dee-ah-da,   Boom-dee-ah-da,   Boom-dee-ah-da.

Música para todos **for Intermediate Grades**

VISUAL AIDS   M•28   Rhythm Patterns

Three Rhythms
(Tres ritmos)

Música para todos for Intermediate Grades

Macmillan/McGraw-Hill

Song Connection

(Canción de la conexión)

Connect the dots from 1 to 9. Put the names of each body part on the line by its number.
Una los puntos del 1 al 9. Escriban el nombre de cada parte del cuerpo al lado del número correspondiente.

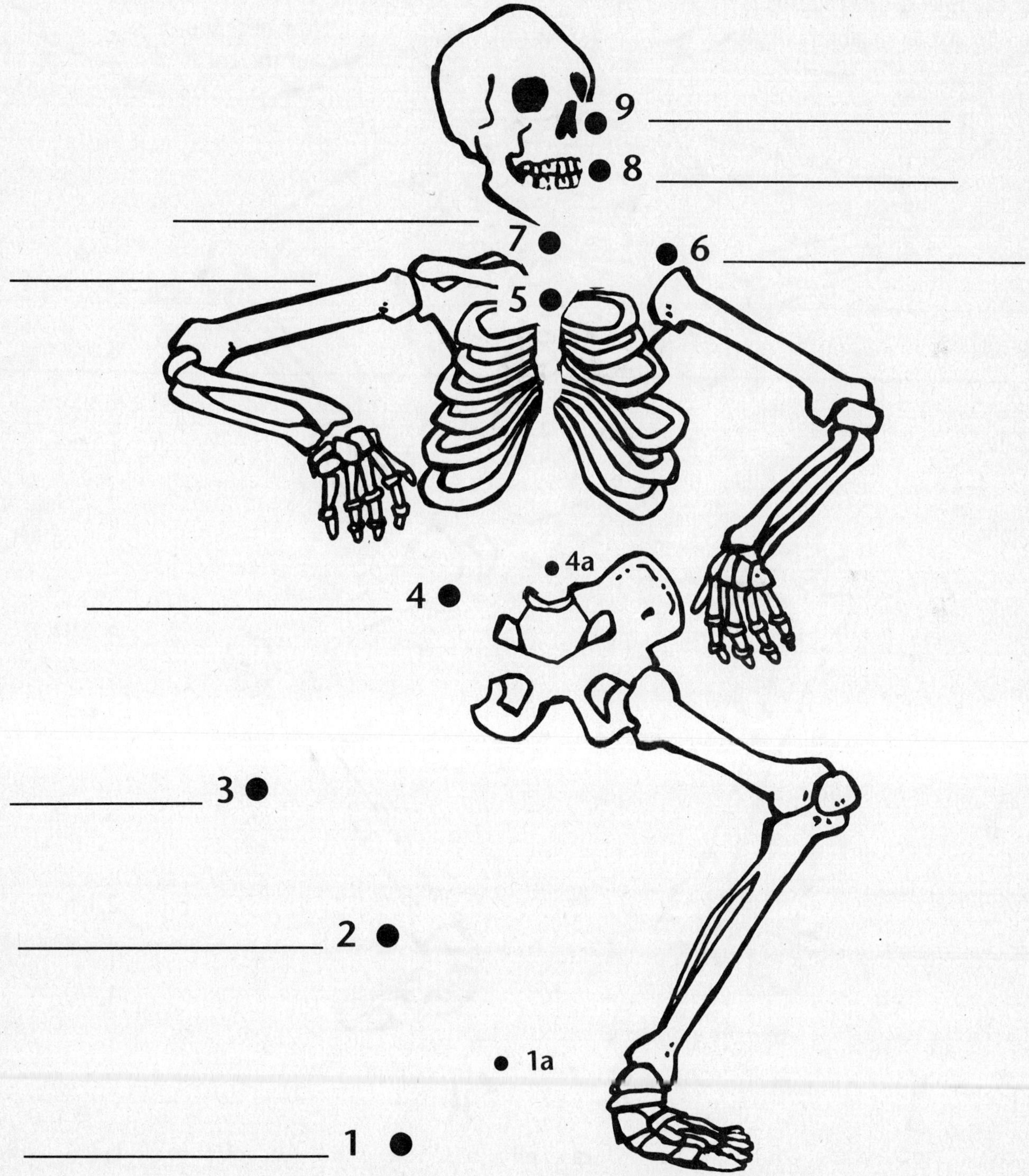

9 _____

8 _____

_____

_____

7

6 _____

5

4a

4 _____

3 _____

2 _____

1a

1 _____

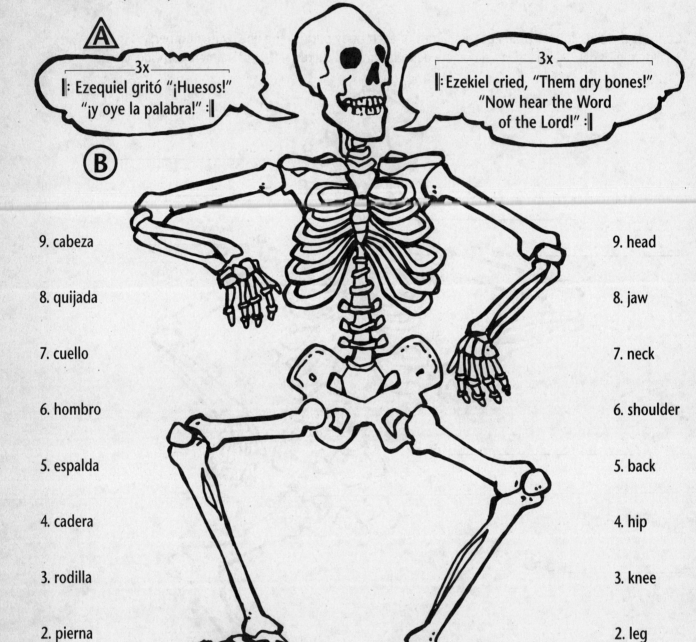

VISUAL AIDS   M•30   Song Map

Dry Bones
(Huesos)

A

3x

‖: Ezequiel gritó "¡Huesos!"
"¡y oye la palabra!" :‖

3x

‖: Ezekiel cried, "Them dry bones!"
"Now hear the Word
of the Lord!" :‖

B

9. cabeza	9. head
8. quijada	8. jaw
7. cuello	7. neck
6. hombro	6. shoulder
5. espalda	5. back
4. cadera	4. hip
3. rodilla	3. knee
2. pierna	2. leg
1. pie	1. foot

sing three times

C

  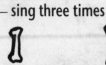

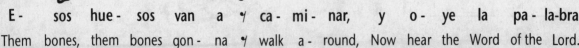

‖: E - sos hue - sos van a ᵧ ca - mi - nar, y o - ye la pa - la-bra :‖
Them bones, them bones gon - na ᵧ walk a - round, Now hear the Word of the Lord.

Música para todos for Intermediate Grades

Name _____

The Ghost of John
(El fantasma de Juan)

¿Han visto
Have you seen

el fantasma
the ghost

de Juan?
of John?

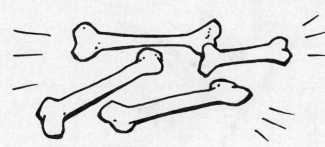

Huesos blancos
Long white bones

sin cutis,
with the skin all gone,

Oo - - - Oo - Oo - Oo - Oo - Oo
Oo - - - Oo - Oo - Oo - Oo - Oo

¡Qué hace frío
Wouldn't it be chilly

sin cutis!
with no skin on!

VISUAL AIDS   M•32   Song Map

Hambone

(Paco)

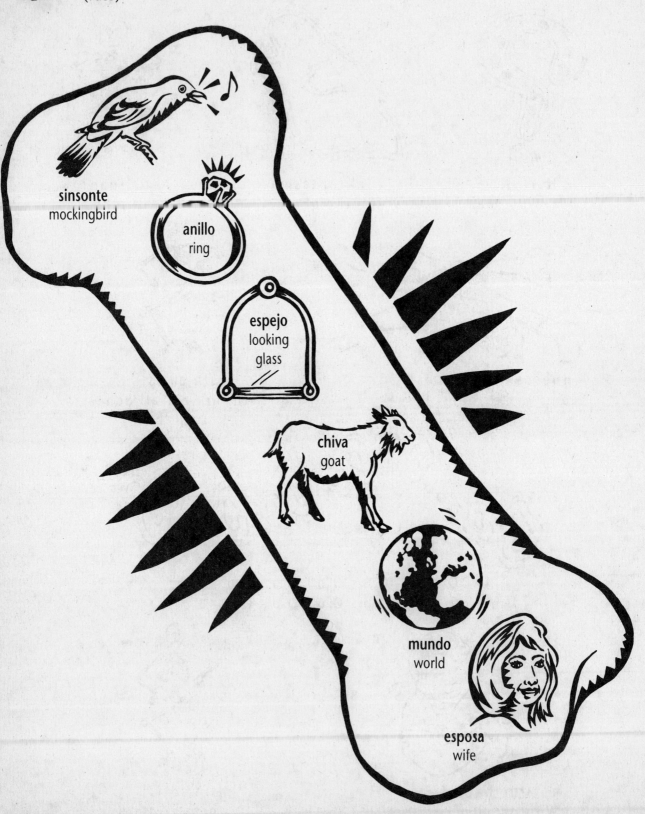

sinsonte
mockingbird

anillo
ring

espejo
looking
glass

chiva
goat

mundo
world

esposa
wife

Música para todos for Intermediate Grades

Name _____

Gift Guide
(Guía de regalos)

Find the rhyming word for each sentence. Sing the new verse.
Busquen una palabra que rime para cada oración. Canten el nuevo verso.

Si la manzana no brilla,
If the apple doesn't shine,
Papi va a comprarme una _____

Si la gorra no me tapa,
If the cap doesn't fit,
Papi va a comprarme una _____

Si la tijera no corta,
If the scissors don't cut,
Papi va a comprarme una _____

Si el creyón no pinta,
If the crayon doesn't color,
Papi va a comprarme una _____

Rhyming words *Palabras que riman*

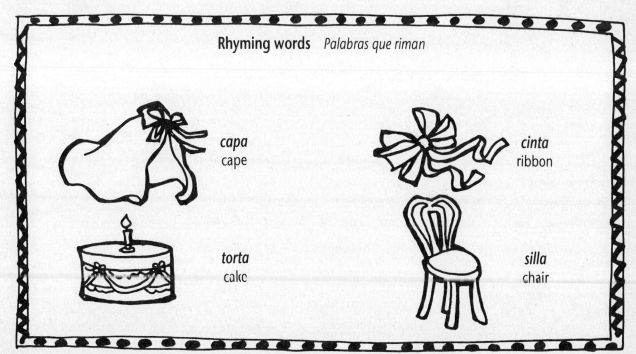

capa
cape

cinta
ribbon

torta
cake

silla
chair

Macmillan/McGraw-Hill

Down the River
(Por el río)

El río está alto

The river is up

el viento sí está fuerte.

The wind is steady and strong.

y el canal profundo,
and the channel is deep,

1. **Ay, qué alegre tiempo tenemos cuando navegamos.**
   Oh, won't we have a jolly good time, As we go sailing along.

2. **Ay, Diana, Diana, cose la torta cuando navegamos.**
   Oh, Dinah, put the hoecake on, As we go sailing along.

3. **Golpea el agua en las orillas cuando navegamos.**
   The waves do splash from shore to shore, As we go sailing along.

Por el río, ay, por el río, ay, por el río a navegar.
Por el río, ay, por el río, ay, por el Río Grande.

Down the river, Oh, down the river, Oh, down the river we go.
Down the river, Oh, down the river, Oh, down the Ohio!

Macmillan/McGraw-Hill

Rhythm Study
(Estudio rítmico)

  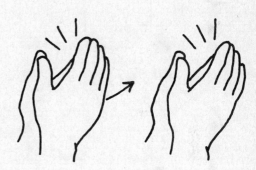

 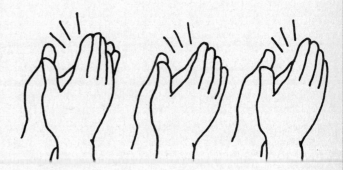

Name _____

VISUAL AIDS   M•36   Flashcards

Favorite Foods
(Comidas favoritas)

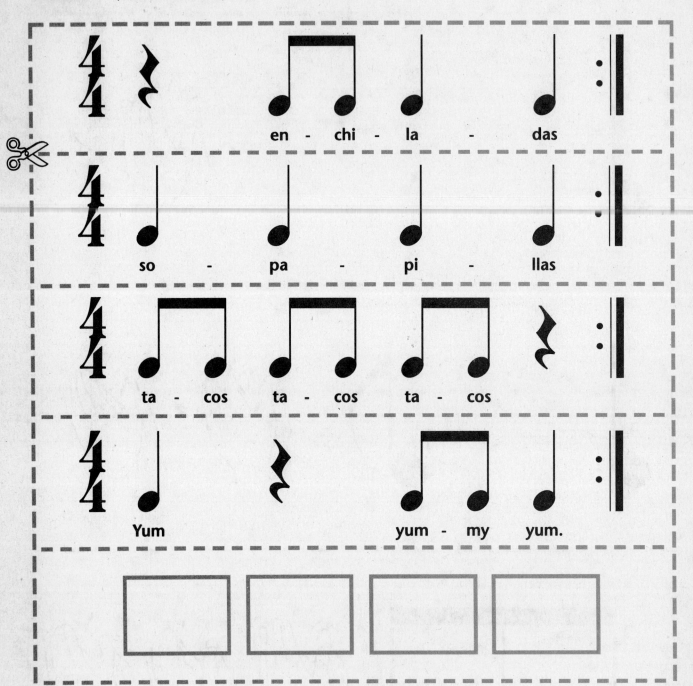

Música para todos for Intermediate Grades

Macmillan/McGraw-Hill

Name _____

Sweet Potatoes
(Camotes dulces)

1

Cocinamos camotes dulces, Los camotes,
  los camotes.
Cocinamos camotes dulces, Comenselos ya.
Soon as we all cook sweet potatoes, sweet
  potatoes, sweet potatoes.
Soon as we all cook sweet potatoes, Eat 'em
  while they're hot.

2

Ya cenados Mami nos llama, Mami llama,
  Mami llama.
Ya cenados Mami nos llama, Váyanse acostar.
Soon as supper's gone, Mamma calls us, Mamma
  calls us, Mamma calls us.
Soon as supper's gone, Mamma calls us, Get
  along to bed.

3

Con la cabeza en la almohada, Almohada,
  almohada,
Con la cabeza en la almohada, Duérmanse ya.
Soon's we touch our heads to the pillow, To the
  pillow,   to the pillow,
Soon's we touch our heads to the pillow, Go to
  sleep right smart!

4

Tan pronto que canta el gallo, Al amanecer,
  al amanecer.
**Tan pronto que canta el gallo, Nos lavamos
  la cara.**
Soon's the rooster crow in the morning, In the
  morning, in the morning.
Soon's the rooster crow in the morning, Gotta
  wash our face.

Macmillan/McGraw-Hill

Charades
(Acertijoz)

Música para todos for Intermediate Grades

Take Time in Life
(Vive la vida)

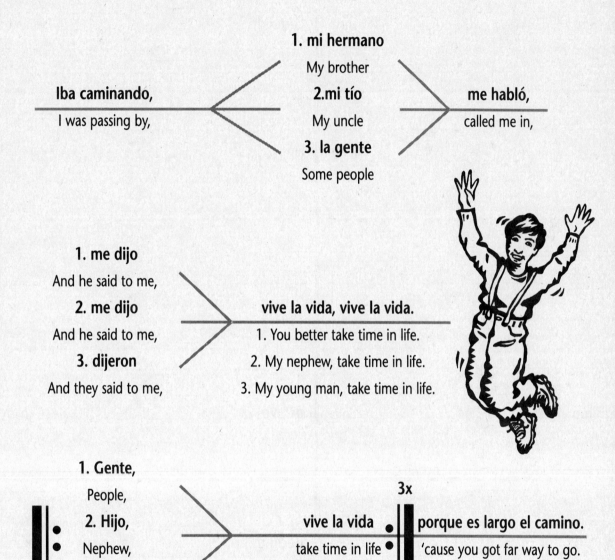

Iba caminando,
I was passing by,

1. mi hermano
My brother

2. mi tío
My uncle

3. la gente
Some people

me habló,
called me in,

1. me dijo
And he said to me,

2. me dijo
And he said to me,

3. dijeron
And they said to me,

vive la vida, vive la vida.
1. You better take time in life.
2. My nephew, take time in life.
3. My young man, take time in life.

1. Gente,
People,

2. Hijo,
Nephew,

3. Joven,
Young man,

vive la vida
take time in life

3x

porque es largo el camino.
'cause you got far way to go.

First to Twelfth
(De primero a duodécimo)

primero	first	**segundo**	second
tercero	third	**cuarto**	fourth
quinto	fifth	**sexto**	sixth
séptimo	seventh	**octavo**	eighth
noveno	ninth	**décimo**	tenth
undécimo	eleventh	**duodécimo**	twelfth

Música para todos for Intermediate Grades

Macmillan/McGraw-Hill

Name _____

Wish List
(Lista de deseos)

Name 12 things you'd like to receive as gifts.
Nombra 12 cosas que te gustaría recibi de regalo.

1. _____

2. _____

3. _____

4. _____

5. _____

6. _____

7. _____

8. _____

9. _____

10. _____

11. _____

12. _____

Use this space to draw a picture of some of the items on your wish list.
Usa este espacio para dibujar algunas de las cosas que están en tu lista de deseos.

Name _____

The Twelve Days of Christmas
(Los doce días de Navidad)

1. **En el primer día después de Navidad, recibí una perdiz en un peral.**
   On the first day of Christmas my true love sent to me: A partridge in a pear tree.

2. **En el segundo día después de Navidad, recibí dos palomitas y una perdiz en un peral.**
   On the second day of Christmas my true love sent to me: Two turtle doves, and a partridge in a pear tree.

3. **En el tercer día . . . tres gallinitas, . . .**
   On the third day . . . Three French hens, . . .

4. **En el cuarto día . . . cuatro gorriones, . . .**
   On the fourth day . . . Four colly birds, . . .

5. **En el quinto día . . . cinco anillos de oro, . . .**
   On the fifth day . . . Five golden rings, . . .

6. **En el sexto día . . . seis lindos gansos, . . .**
   On the sixth day . . . Six geese a-laying, . . .

Música para todos for Intermediate Grades

The Twelve Days of Christmas

(Los doce días de Navidad)

7.   En el séptimo día . . . siete cisnes, . . .
On the seventh day . . . Seven swans a-swimming, . . .

8.   En el octavo día . . . ocho lecheras, . . .
On the eighth day . . . Eight maids a-milking, . . .

9.   En el noveno día . . . nueve tamborileros, . . .
On the ninth day . . . Nine drummers drumming, . . .

10.   En el décimo día . . . diez flautistas, . . .
On the tenth day . . . Ten pipers piping, . . .

11.   En el undécimo día . . . once bailarinas, . . .
On the eleventh day . . . Eleven ladies dancing, . . .

12.   En el duodécimo día . . . doce saltadores, . . .
On the twelfth day . . . Twelve lords a-leaping, . . .

Celebration
(Celebración)

Música para todos for Intermediate Grades

Name _____

Auld Lang Syne
(El calor de la amistad)

Verso 1 / Verse 1

1.

¿Olvidarás nuestra amistad
Should auld acquaintance be forgot,

y el tiempo pasado?
{ And never brought to mind?
{ And days of auld lang syne?

Estribillo / Refrain:

Adiós, adiós, amigo fiel,
For auld land syne, my dear,

pero aquí siempre quedará
We'll tak' a cup o' kindness yet,

Muy pronto he de partir,
For auld lang syne;

el calor de la amistad.
For auld lang syne.

Verso 2 / Verse 2

2. Toma mi mano amigo
And here's a hand, my trusty frien',

una tacita de bondad
We'll tak' a cup o' kindness yet,

y tú me la darás
And gie's a hand o' thine;

por nuestra amistad.
For auld lang syne.

Name _____

VISUAL AIDS   M•45   Cue Cards

Time to Go

(Hora de irse)

12:15

12:20

12:25

12:30

12:45

12:55

Música para todos for Intermediate Grades

Macmillan/McGraw-Hill

Using the El carnavalito *Script*

SCENERY, COSTUME, AND PROP IDEAS

SCENERY

The backdrop, which can be painted on butcher paper, shows a carnival scene, with game booths, food stands, a Ferris wheel and other rides, and so on. A sign reading, "Carnival! One day only!" should be prominently displayed on the backdrop or as a separate prop.

If there is no stage or curtain, the backdrop can be rolled up and down, as needed. Lights can be turned on and off during scene changes, while stagehands move the few pieces of furniture. Or changes can simply be made with the lights on.

COSTUMES

Paco, his friends, Luz, small children, and carnival attendees all wear contemporary clothing. Paco's father and Señora Sánchez wear age-appropriate casual clothes; Paco's mother wears a business suit. The dancer wears a beautiful folk dance costume (such as a white, peasant-style blouse with a wide, colorful skirt) and has a flower in her hair. The vendor and the fishmonger can both wear the same type of butcher-style apron.

PROPS

5 backpacks

Soccer ball

Leaflet

Table (with tablecloth) set for dinner for four, with dishes, silverware, and a couple of serving bowls

4 chairs

Large platter of food or roasting pan

Folding bed or cot

White candles for *La cumbia* dancers

Pasteles booth (Use dinner table and tablecloth, with same platter and/or one or two rectangular roasting pans on it. A pile of napkins is on one side. A sign says, "*Pasteles,* $1.00.")

Fake dollar bills

Photograph

4 fishing poles (can be made from sticks and string)

4 strings of (paper) fish

Oversized book with skeleton pictured on the cover

Skeleton hanging from a pole (or painted on butcher paper)

Eye chart

Cleaning supplies: feather duster, rag, broom, and dustpan (used by Julio and later by Paco)

Chirping bird (sound effect)

Brightly colored balloons (optional: additional carnival souvenirs or foods such as fake ice cream, cotton candy)

MOVEMENT

Encourage students to create their own movements for all songs that do not have movement instructions in the script.

MUSIC

Take Time in Life (Vive la vida), page 51, Spanish **CD2:20;** Pronunciation **CD2:21;** English **CD2:22**

For Health and Strength (Salud y fuerza), page 33, Spanish **CD1:28;** Pronunciation **CD1:29;** English **CD1:30**

La cumbia, page 3, **CD1:1;** Pronunciation **CD1:2**

Si me dan pasteles (When You Bring *Pasteles*), page 19, Spanish/English **CD1:15;** Pronunciation **CD1:16;** Performance Mix **CD1:17**

Down the River (Por el río), page 45, Spanish **CD2:13;** Pronunciation **CD2:14;** English **CD2:15;** Performance Mix **CD2:16**

Dry Bones (Huesos), page 37, Spanish **CD2:4;** Pronunciation **CD2:5;** English **CD2:6**

Chíu, chíu, chíu, page 13, Spanish/English **CD1:11;** Pronunciation **CD1:12**

De colores (Many Colors), page 27, Spanish **CD1:21;** Pronunciation **CD1:22;** English **CD1:23**

Auld Lang Syne (El calor de la amistad), page 57, Spanish **CD2:26;** Pronunciation **CD2:27;** English **CD2:28**

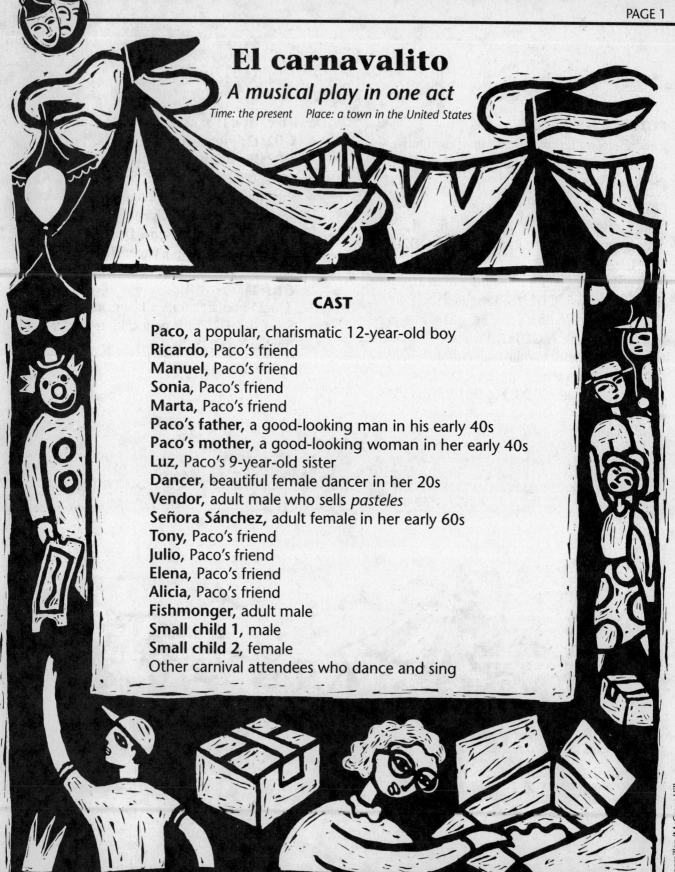

El carnavalito

A musical play in one act

Time: the present   Place: a town in the United States

CAST

Paco, a popular, charismatic 12-year-old boy
Ricardo, Paco's friend
Manuel, Paco's friend
Sonia, Paco's friend
Marta, Paco's friend
Paco's father, a good-looking man in his early 40s
Paco's mother, a good-looking woman in her early 40s
Luz, Paco's 9-year-old sister
Dancer, beautiful female dancer in her 20s
Vendor, adult male who sells *pasteles*
Señora Sánchez, adult female in her early 60s
Tony, Paco's friend
Julio, Paco's friend
Elena, Paco's friend
Alicia, Paco's friend
Fishmonger, adult male
Small child 1, male
Small child 2, female
Other carnival attendees who dance and sing

SCENE I

(Paco, a charismatic 12-year-old and the most popular boy in the sixth grade, is onstage kicking around a soccer ball on his way home from school. Lying nearby is his backpack. His classmates, Sonia, Ricardo, Manuel, and Marta, enter as a group, discussing a leaflet Sonia has in her hands. They see Paco.)

Manuel: Hey Paco, my main man! *(He and Ricardo give Paco high fives.)*

Paco: ¡Hola Ricardo, Manuel! Marta. *(He nods hello to her.)* What's that, Sonia?

Sonia: They were giving these out in front of school. There's going to be a carnival tomorrow! One day only! With games, a Ferris wheel, a gravitron ... *(She hands Paco the leaflet.)*

Paco *(reading the leaflet):* That's awesome. *Tenemos que ir.* We have to go. We deserve a good time, especially after all the work Mr. Fuentes has been loading on us lately. *(Others voice their agreement.)*

SONG *(Paco, Ricardo, Manuel, Sonia, Marta):* **"Take Time in Life"** **(Vive la vida)**

(As Paco sings the first two phrases, he puts his arm around his "brother" Ricardo. All join in on the third and fourth phrases of each verse. This pattern continues, with Manuel as the "uncle" in the second verse and the two girls as "some people" in the third verse.)

Paco: We have to get a whole group together. It'll be the party of the year, man! *Hablemos a Tony, Julio, José ...*

Marta: ... María, Elena, Alicia ... *(At the mention of Alicia, Ricardo and Manuel start teasing Paco, as if they think he likes her.)*

Paco *(grinning):* Be cool, dudes. She's just a friend! *(The other kids all shake their heads and look cynical.)* Anyway, tomorrow after the game we'll pick a time and place for everyone to meet. *(Paco picks up his backpack and ball and they all walk offstage talking excitedly about the carnival.)*

SCENE II

(In the background is a backdrop showing a carnival scene. Upstage left is a table with four chairs. Upstage right is a bed. Seated at the table, which is set for dinner, are Paco, his mother, and his younger sister, Luz, called Lucie. His father walks in from the left carrying a platter or roasting pan with dinner, which he puts on the table. He sits down; all sing "For Health and Strength" as a two-part round.)

SONG *(Paco, father, mother, Luz):* **"For Health and Strength" (Salud y fuerza)**

Father: *¡A comer!* Let's eat! *(All begin eating.)*

Paco: How was work today, Mom?

Mother: Pretty good. One of my students won a National Merit Scholarship, and we had a little party in class to celebrate. *(smiling)* Must be because he had such a great math teacher. *(Others agree; Paco "slaps her five.")* How was your day, Paco?

Paco: Great. Tomorrow a whole bunch of us are going to that carnival that just arrived in town. Have you heard about it? They even have a gravitron!

Father: *Pero Paco ...*

Paco *(smiling):* No, no way am I taking Lucie with me and my friends! *(Luz makes a face at him.)*

Mother: That's not the problem, dear. Don't you remember, you promised to help Señora Sánchez clean out her garage and pack up all the stuff there? She's leaving for Arizona on Sunday to go and live with her daughter and grandkids ...

Paco *(getting defensive):* Well, she'll have to leave on Monday instead.

Father: Paco, you know she can't do that. She already has her plane ticket. And besides, her granddaughter won a role in a City Ballet production, and she promised to be there for her debut. You know that granddaughter is the joy of her life, especially since Señor Sánchez died.

Paco *(glaring):* I'm not going to miss the social event of the year because of anybody's old garage!

Mother *(quietly):* Señora Sánchez is not just "anybody," Paco. She was your baby-sitter for eleven years! Remember last year when you couldn't find that science report ...

Luz: ... she stayed here till midnight helping you rewrite it.

Father: Yes, and remember the time she taught you long division when you felt you couldn't keep up with the class, how she made *sopa de pollo* for you every time you were sick ...

Paco *(jumps up):* I don't care!

(Paco runs across the stage and sits down, sulking, on his bed. His family exits stage left. The lights go out. Stagehands remove the dinner table and the chairs.)

SCENE III

(When the lights go on again, Paco is lying in his bed, getting ready to go to sleep.)

Paco: I can't wait 'til tomorrow. Maybe I'll ask Alicia to ride the Ferris wheel with me. *(He yawns and stretches, then closes his eyes and goes to sleep. What follows is a dream sequence.)*

Dancer *(a dreamy offstage voice is calling him):* Paco, Paco!

Paco *(groggily):* But it's not time to wake up yet. It's only midnight.

(A woman, dressed in a folk dance costume, enters downstage left and walks gracefully toward Paco's bed.)

Dancer: ¡Paco, ven! Come to the carnival! ¡Ven a bailar la cumbia conmigo! Come dance *la cumbia* with me!

Paco: But I don't know how! And besides, I have to ...

Dancer: *Yo te enseñaré.* I will teach you. *(She takes his hand and pulls him up off the bed.)*

SONG *(all):* "La cumbia"

(The dancer holds an unlit candle and dances a shuffling step while Paco moves in a zigzag pattern around her. After the first verse they are joined in the dance by Sonia and Ricardo, and Marta and Manuel, who greet Paco using gestures. Other dancing couples join them as well. Everyone dances, clapping their hands at the end, all in pantomime. A vendor wearing an apron enters upstage left, carrying or

wheeling in the dinner table with platters of pasteles *on it and a sign saying, "Pasteles, $1.00." The dancer curtsies and exits stage left. The other couples, with the exception of Paco's friends, move on toward the* pasteles *vendor and pantomime purchasing some to eat.)*

Vendor: *¡Pasteles!* Nice and hot!

Paco *(to his friends):* I love *pasteles!* All that dancing has made me hungry. Besides *(starts looking guilty),* I didn't eat much dinner last night ... *(They walk over to the vendor, who hands Paco a* pastele *in a napkin. Paco pays him for it. His friends follow suit, all in pantomime. The other dancers are milling around, eating* pasteles *or pantomiming playing carnival games.)*

SONG *(all):* **"Si me dan pasteles" (When You Bring** *Pasteles***)**

(Señora Sánchez enters from downstage right and walks over to the booth. Everyone stops what they are doing to silently watch and react to the dialogue between Paco and Señora Sánchez.)

Señora Sánchez: So there you are, Paco! *¡Así que estás aquí, Paco!*

Paco *(looks stricken):* Hola, *Señora Sánchez.*

Señora Sánchez: When you didn't show up today, I figured you'd be here instead.

Paco: *Lo siento.* I'm sorry, but ...

Señora Sánchez *(with a big sigh): Está bien.* I told my grand-daughter I'd be coming down next week instead. She was disappointed, but she promised to send me a photo of her on stage in her costume. *Imagina,* only eight years old and chosen from all of the ballet schools in Tucson. ... Have I shown you her recent school picture? *(She takes out a photograph and shows him. Everyone indicates approval.)*

Paco *(feeling terrible): Es muy linda.* You must be very proud.

Señora Sánchez *(with another big sigh): Sí.* Bueno, adiós, Paco. I'll miss you and your sister when I move to Tucson. You always were such a sweet boy. *(Paco's friends and the other dancers are glaring at him angrily. After Señora Sánchez exits stage left, his friends stalk off in a huff, stage right, followed by the other dancers who are shaking their heads with disapproval.)*

Paco: *Sonia, Marta, Manuel, Ricky, ¡Esperen!*

(The vendor takes his table and exits stage left. Paco goes back to bed, lies down, then wakes up abruptly. He is trembling.)

Paco *(to the audience):* What a horrible dream I just had!

(The lights go out. The bed is removed from the stage.)

SCENE IV

(Paco and his friends—boys and girls—are playing soccer, in pantomime. Paco scores a goal. His friends all jump up and cheer, surrounding him and patting him on the back.)

Tony: Great goal, Paco!

Julio: So what time should we meet today?

Paco *(depressed):* I can't go.

Tony: What do you mean, you can't go? *¿Hay algún problema?*

Paco: It's a long story. But you guys have a great time. *(He runs off, stage right.)*

Elena: *¡Qué pena!* It just won't be the same without Paco!

Alicia: I wonder what the problem is.

Tony: Maybe since his father got laid off last month, they don't have the money ...

Julio: I bet that's it.

Elena: It's still early. If we all found some jobs ...

Alicia: ... we could earn enough money to take Paco to the fair! *(They all murmur agreement.)* *¡Vamos!* We can meet back at Paco's house at 3:00. *(They all exit.)*

SCENE V

(Ricardo, Manuel, Sonia, and Marta are sitting on the edge of the stage, in front of the curtain, downstage left, holding fishing poles. They sing "Down the River," dividing into parts for the refrain.)

SONG *(Ricardo, Manuel, Sonia, Marta):*   **"Down the River"** **(Por el río)**

(They all pantomime fishing. At the end of the song each one holds up several fish on a string. A fishmonger enters and, in pantomime, offers

them money for the fish. As the man pays them, the four turn to the audience and smile. They go back to fishing.

Alicia enters, stage right, with two small children in tow, holding an oversized book with a picture of a skeleton on the cover. They sit down on the floor, center stage, facing the audience. During the song Alicia pantomimes reading the words to the song from the book, perhaps pointing to the picture of the skeleton on the cover.

Tony, Julio, and Elena enter stage right. Tony is carrying a large eye examination chart, which he hangs on the curtain, and a feather duster. Elena is wheeling in a skeleton on a pole and holds a cleaning rag in the other hand. Julio carries in a broom and dustpan. All three pantomime cleaning the doctor's office as they sing "Dry Bones." Elena "cleans" each bone on the skeleton as it is mentioned in the song.)

SONG *(Tony, Julio, Elena, Alicia, small children):* **"Dry Bones" (Huesos)**

(At the end of the song the boys and the fishmonger exit stage left, and the girls and children exit stage right, carrying their props.)

SCENE VI

(The curtain opens on a bare stage with the carnival backdrop. Paco is standing alone, with a broom and dustpan in his hands, looking off-stage, listening to a bird chirp. He is very sad.)

SONG *(Paco):* **"Chíu, chíu, chíu"**

(Paco's friends rush onstage, calling his name.)

Ricardo: ¡Paco, mira! Look what we have! *(He hands him a bunch of dollars in a rubber band.)* Now you can go to the carnival with us!

Paco: Where did you get this?

Manuel: We all worked for it.

Alicia: Those Rivera twins made me read the same book to them five times!

Marta: We thought maybe you weren't going to the carnival because you didn't have the money.

Paco *(very moved):* I can't believe you did this for me. *(pauses)* But the reason I couldn't go is that I promised to help Señora Sánchez today, and I couldn't let her down.

Tony: What do you have to do?

Macmillan/McGraw-Hill

Paco: Clean out her garage and pack her stuff up. She's moving to Arizona tomorrow.

Julio: If we all helped ...

Elena: ... we could be done in no time! *(All nod agreement.)*

Sonia: What are we waiting for? *¡Vamos!* *(They all run off, stage left.)*

SCENE VII

(The dancers from Paco's dream are milling around, enjoying the carnival. Paco and his friends enter stage left, carrying brightly colored balloons and other carnival items, such as cotton candy, and chattering excitedly.)

SONG *(all):* **"De colores" (Many Colors)**

(Paco's father, mother, and sister, also carrying balloons, enter stage right and greet Paco and his friends.)

Father: So, Paco, what did you decide to do?

Paco: Because my friends helped me, I was able to help Señora Sánchez *and* go to the carnival!

Father: And thanks to *my* friends, I was able to locate a good job with the new engineering firm opening up down the road.

Paco *(to his friends):* Speaking of help, what are you going to do with all the money you earned?

Julio: Maybe we could donate it to the homeless shelter ...

Alicia: ... or the free clinic where I do volunteer work.

Mother: When people work together, everyone benefits. *Tenemos suerte de tener tan buenos amigos.* We're all lucky to have so many wonderful friends.

SONG *(all):* **"Auld Lang Syne" (El calor de la amistad)**

I. ARE YOU CULTURALLY SENSITIVE?
An Informal Checklist

Use the following questions to assess your cultural sensitivity.

CLASSROOM ATMOSPHERE

YES	SOMETIMES	NO	
☐	☐	☐	• Do you discuss your own cultural heritage with students?
☐	☐	☐	• Do you know the cultural backgrounds of your students?
☐	☐	☐	• Are you interested in knowing how your students' cultural backgrounds influence their values, beliefs, and understanding of the world?
☐	☐	☐	• Do you let your students teach you what you didn't know or understand about their cultures?
☐	☐	☐	• Do you discuss with students the impact that culture has on our lives?
☐	☐	☐	• Do you work to clarify misconceptions, negative beliefs, and stereotypes about people from diverse cultures, ethnic groups, and religions?
☐	☐	☐	• Are you aware of your own stereotypes?
☐	☐	☐	• Are you on your guard against letting your stereotypes interfere with your students' academic and personal growth?

CLASSROOM CONTENT AND INSTRUCTION

YES	SOMETIMES	NO	
☐	☐	☐	• Do you take into consideration that students with different cultural backgrounds may have different learning styles and may respond to some approaches or activities better than others?
☐	☐	☐	• Do you use appropriate assessment techniques, especially ones that allow for a variety of learning styles?
☐	☐	☐	• Do you help students to see that events and issues can be viewed from a variety of perspectives?
☐	☐	☐	• Do you encourage students to explore various perspectives when thinking through an issue or problem?
☐	☐	☐	• Do you review materials you use in the classroom to be certain they are culturally sensitive and accurate?
☐	☐	☐	• Do you provide materials for students to read that are written by and/or about people from culturally diverse backgrounds?
☐	☐	☐	• Are your curricula—especially language arts, social studies, and the arts—grounded in multiculturalism? That is, is multiculturalism central to the content/instruction rather than simply added on or addressed from time to time?

II. STUDENTS ACQUIRING A SECOND LANGUAGE

A popular misconception regarding multicultural education is that it is intended primarily or exclusively for minority students. . . . Because all students ultimately will need to function in our culturally diverse society, all should be exposed to educational experiences that foster the necessary competencies for doing so. (Hernández, Hilda. *Multicultural Education: A Teacher's Guide to Content and Processes.* Columbus, Ohio: Merrill, 1989.)

Wong Fillmore (1976) found that the amount of time a child requires to become a proficient user of the second language has been greatly underestimated. She concludes that most children require from four to six years to become competent users of English. For some children, it may take as long as five to eight years.

Students are likely to learn best in instructional environments that are consistent with their learning-style preferences. For this reason, teachers faced with culturally diverse classes and students who differ in their learning preferences must be able to draw upon a variety of teaching strategies appropriate to various learning styles. (Hernández, 1989)

How do I help a student acquire a second language?

- Use a lot of repetition. Say and do things many times in one class period and on subsequent days.
- Present your lesson in small "chunks" of information. Progress from easy to more difficult in small increments. For example, have students sing just the repeated phrase of a song before asking them to sing the entire chorus. Then have them begin learning a verse.
- Select concepts and vocabulary that you want every student to master, and give those items increased emphasis by using repetition. Target two or three key words in each lesson. Work primarily toward helping students to start singing and secondarily toward giving them an idea of the content.
- Label classroom objects and equipment (door=*puerta*; chairs=*sillas*; third grade books=*libros de tercer grado*, and so on).
- Acknowledge and praise or validate all student responses.

What are some techniques for presenting information to students acquiring a second language?

- Use a variety of teaching approaches in order to include all learning styles. Include small-group, large-group, aural, kinesthetic, and visual activities in your lesson.
- Use silent signal directions when possible.
- Act out words and emphasize meaning with your voice. Use movement to bring meaning to words whenever possible. Ham it up! (examples: Clap on accented syllables; raise arms in air for high/*alto*, and so on.)
- Use visuals that have both pictures and words, in Spanish and English. Point to appropriate pictures as you go along.
- Use other school materials and resources such as library books and filmstrips to aid the students in acquiring more background information on the vocabulary or song.
- Speak and give directions at a slower tempo than you would for single-language classes. Use a clear, slow speaking voice in a high or medium range, avoiding a monotone or low speaking range. Keep sentences relatively short and simple. Sing directions whenever possible to add musical interest and to encourage listening.
- Ask single-response questions that can be answered with *yes*, *no,* or another one-word answer to provide opportunities for success.

How do I accommodate language differences in my classroom?

- Seat a student acquiring a second language next to a native speaker to provide a good role model and a "buddy."
- Have students follow with their fingers when using a textbook or an individual copy of a song map. (example: On a song map, have them point to the picture that represents each phrase while singing that phrase.)
- Be aware of and point out cross-language homonyms—words that sound the same in both languages. (examples: colors=*colores*; train=*tren*; circle=*círculo*; music=*música*; chocolate=*chocolate*; pillars=*pilares*)
- Summarize material periodically throughout the lesson and relate it to the objective of the lesson.
- Elaborate on what the student acquiring a second language says by restating and adding additional meaning and information.
- Make meaning a priority; pronunciation and sentence structure will improve in due course.

- Have the same expectations for students who are acquiring a second language that you have for your native speakers. When provided with adequate instruction, their skill development should be equal to that of their peers. The only exception to this is when language is a barrier to their being able to tell you what they have learned. Leveling down for students who are acquiring a second language is an inappropriate teaching technique.

How do I work to improve students' production of sounds and words?

- Listen to students' diction as well as to rhythmic and melodic accuracy, intonation, and other aspects of musicality. Correct diction when appropriate by rephrasing or repeating the problem words or sounds.
- Watch for students who exhibit difficulty with aural discrimination. Students who mispronounce words may not be hearing them correctly.
- Set up a listening center in which students may listen to and practice with recorded pronunciations and songs.
- Have students tape-record themselves in their native and second languages.
- Allow students ample time to pronounce the words in the context of the lesson. Use the words in the rhythmic context of the song.
- Use the recording while pointing to the vocabulary words on the board.
- Have native speakers lead students acquiring a second language in saying the words.
- Remind students to look at your mouth for the pronunciation of difficult words.
- Avoid overdoing pronunciation practice. Limit to about three the number of times students practice the words, and let the song teach the words.

How can I help promote a sense of positive self-esteem and belonging for students acquiring a second language?

- Plan a review of familiar material for every music lesson (a song or a movement activity with which students are comfortable). This provides students with a sense of security and success. Structure your lessons around a routine that students will become familiar with, again providing them with security that will enhance motivation.
- Show respect for the students' native languages by pronouncing names correctly.
- Use greetings with unchanging texts. (example: *Buenos días, niños*— Good day, everyone.)

Macmillan/McGraw-Hill

- Assign classroom duties to the student acquiring a second language to increase involvement and responsibility. (examples: page turner, material distributor/collector)
- Sing songs in an unfamiliar third language or use sign language, thus putting all students on equal experience and ability levels.
- Learn about the non-native speaker's culture and show respect for it by including information on it in your lessons. Promote cultural diversity by making it a part of your lessons and challenging students to learn about each other and about cultures not represented in their class.
- Acknowledge and praise student responses and participation.

III. *MÚSICA PARA TODOS* LESSONS

How much time do I spend teaching the songs?

- Allow more than one class period to work on learning the vocabulary words and the song before teaching the lesson objective.

How do I help students learn the songs?

- Have students listen to the entire recording before they learn the song.
- Sing the song at a slower tempo than the recording to allow students time to practice using their new vocabulary. After two or three tries at the slower tempo, challenge students to sing the song up to tempo with the recording. If they are unable to sing the entire song correctly, slow the tempo again, then try the faster tempo after two more tries. (Always singing the song at a slower tempo will keep students at that tempo. The challenge gives them a frame of reference as to how much longer they will need to work with the words and melody to perform them at the correct tempo.)
- Provide a copy of the song sheet and make the recording available to other teachers to use in their classroom centers.
- Provide checkout packets of the songs.
- Separate the melody from the words by using vocalises to correct problems. (example: Sing on *la* or *loo*, or hum the song.)
- Preview song maps with students, noting where the song begins (not always at the top), key words and pictures, and where the song ends, as well as the title of the song.

What are some ways to teach key vocabulary?

- Provide students with frequent opportunities to see and hear the words. Frequent repetition and practice will aid them in learning the words.
- List all vocabulary words on the board using large letters so they can be read from the back of the room. Use care with handwriting. Avoid mixing lowercase and uppercase letters.
- Use color on the chalkboard to stimulate interest.
- When possible, use pictures with the vocabulary words.
- Use a great deal of voice inflection to emphasize words and syllables. Add movements, gestures, or pantomime to emphasize the meaning of the words or accented syllables.
- Echo-say the song, first with you as the leader, then with a student as the leader. (Choose a student leader who is a native speaker.)

- Introduce the words a few at a time in the context of the song. Associate the vocabulary with objects and materials in the classroom and experiences in the students' lives.
- Use questioning techniques, brainstorming, and predictions to provide practice with the words. For example, have students fill in the blanks to complete song phrases: *¿Quién tiene el ____ (peso)?* or *El río está ____ (alto)*. Or, have them predict what a word means.
- Use bulletin boards to display vocabulary words.
- Make vocabulary-word charts to display for each lesson as needed. Make vocabulary-word card sets for student use. Include both Spanish and English.
- Put the vocabulary words and song maps in a listening station for students to review and practice with the recording. Include hand puppets and visuals as a way to help students practice saying the words or singing the song.

What are some techniques for having students practice vocabulary?

- Allow students time to pronounce the words several times, especially on their first exposure.
- When possible, use "Language Master" strips with the vocabulary words on them. (A "Language Master" machine includes blank strips that can be written on with a transparency pen. The teacher is able to record sounds into the machine for playback. The strip is inserted into a slot, which engages the playback mode, and the listener is able to view the word while hearing it pronounced.) Have students practice saying the recorded words by listening on headphones. You may choose to have students write their own words, record their voices into the machine, and repeat the words with their recording.
- Set up a center with a tape recorder and blank tape for students to record themselves practicing vocabulary words.
- Use vocabulary flashcards in whole- or small-group settings for students to practice saying and singing song words.
- Use varying vocabulary-pronunciation practices, such as recitations, skits, dramas, group practice, and individual practices.

Q When a lesson calls for small-group work, what do I do to involve all members of the group?

A
- Provide a time line to aid groups in staying on task and not lingering too long on any given step in the assignment. As students work, give time reminders as to where they should be.
- Assign everyone a job. (examples: writer, timekeeper, encourager, moderator, spokesperson)

Q How can I modify assessment procedures to insure an accurate measurement of the knowledge of students acquiring a second language?

A
- Practice the assessment activity as a class before giving it individually.
- On a performance assessment, seat the student acquiring a second language near yourself or a reliable, bilingual student who can give key words in Spanish on how to complete the requirements. (examples: when to play the instrument, when to sing, and so on)
- When assessing, be sensitive to questions or instructions that present barriers to students acquiring a second language; however, learning expectations should be the same for all students.
- Address a variety of learning styles when assessing learning. Include visual, aural, and kinesthetic response opportunities.

IV. VISUAL AIDS

 How can I use color to enhance my use of transparencies with students acquiring a second language?

- Use color to highlight form. (examples: verses = red; refrain = blue)
- Use color to mark same/different phrases and/or melodies.
- Use color to draw attention to musical controls.
  (examples: ⌒ = orange, $\|\colon\|$ = green, *p* = yellow, *f* = blue)
- Use color to add interest, to highlight key vocabulary words, and to illustrate words. (examples: sun = yellow; heart = red)
- Color song titles to highlight them.
- Use *erasable* transparency markers when you are having each class give input that will be marked directly on a transparency.
- Use *permanent* markers for adding color that you will use as a part of every lesson and for coloring items you will not need to change from class to class.
- Use *erasable* markers on the front side of a transparency; use permanent markers on the back side, as some transparency print will smear when colored over.

 How can I make most effective use of the overhead projector?

- If possible, leave the lights on. Most overhead projectors are designed to be used without having the room darkened.
- Use a pointer such as a beverage stirrer or pen with a cap on to follow the song map or direct students to a particular item on a transparency.
- Make sure students can see around you and around/over the projector when you are at the projector.
- Check the focus and positioning of the transparency on the screen frequently.
- Have the screen at an appropriate level for students—too high, near the ceiling, will cause them discomfort; too low will block the view of some students.
- When teaching a song from an overhead, use a sheet of paper to cover lines of words or phrases that have not yet been introduced. Slowly reveal the other lines to allow students to focus on small segments at a time.
- After using a transparency, provide copies for student review. Have students point to the pictures and/or words as they sing.

V. MUSIC TEACHING TERMS AND TRANSLATIONS

A list of music vocabulary with translations is included, to be used in conjunction with the lessons or as a tool for general instruction.

INSTRUMENTS / *INSTRUMENTOS*

Instruments of the Orchestra / *Instrumentos de la orquesta*

Brass Instruments / *Instrumentos de metal*

French horn	*trompa*	trumpet	*trompeta*
trombone	*trombón*	tuba	*tuba*

Percussion Instruments / *Instrumentos de percusión*

cymbal	*címbalo*	tambourine	*pandereta*
cymbals	*platillos*	triangle	*triángulo*
drum	*tambor*	xylophone	*xilófono*
piano	*piano*		

String Instruments / *Instrumentos de cuerda*

cello	*violoncelo*	viola	*viola*
double bass	*contrabajo*	violin	*violín*
harp	*arpa*		

Woodwind Instruments / *Instrumentos de viento*

bassoon	*fagot*	oboe	*oboe*
clarinet	*clarinete*	piccolo	*flautín*
English horn	*corno inglés*	saxophone	*saxofón*
flute	*flauta*		

Folk Instruments / *Instrumentos de música folklórica*

banjo	*banjo*	guitar	*guitarra*
fiddle	*violín*	harmonica	*armónica*

Mariachi Instruments / *Instrumentos de los mariachis*

guitar	*guitarra*	small guitar	*guitarra de golpe*
large guitar	*guitarrón*	smallest guitar	*vihuela*

Classroom Instruments /	güiro	*güiro*	rhythm sticks	*palitos de ritmo*
Instrumentos del salón	jingle bells	*cascabeles*	sand block	*"sand block"*
de clases	keyboard	*teclado*	triangle	*triángulo*
	mallets	*martillos*	woodblock	*"woodblock"*
	recorder	*flauta dulce*		

Parts of the Instruments /	bell (as a	*pabellón*	mouthpiece	*boquilla*
Partes de instrumentos	part of an		neck	*mástil*
	instrument)		pedal	*pedal*
	bow	*arco*	pegs	*clavijas*
	double reed	*lengüeta doble*	reed	*lengüeta de caña*
	key	*tecla*	string	*cuerda*

Instrument-Playing	to bow (violin)	*tocar con el arco*	to scrape	*raspar*
Techniques / *Técnicas*	to pluck	*puntear*	to shake	*agitar*
instrumentales	to ring	*tocar*	to strike	*golpear*
	to rub	*frotar*	to tap	*dar golpes ligeros*

MUSIC ELEMENTS AND RELATED TERMS / ELEMENTOS MUSICALES Y TÉRMINOS RELACIONADOS

beat	*compás*	melody	*melodía*
different	*diferente*	note	*nota*
down	*abajo*	rhythm	*ritmo*
fast	*rápido*	same	*igual, lo mismo*
in tune	*afinado*	scale	*escala*
key	*clave*	slow	*despacio*
legato	*legato*	smooth	*suave*
line	*línea*	tempo	*tempo*
loud	*fuerte*	up	*arriba*
medium loud	*fuerte mediano*	very loud	*muy fuerte*
medium soft	*suave mediano*	very soft	*muy suave*

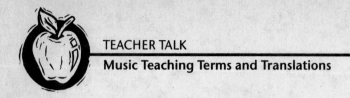

PERFORMERS AND PERFORMANCES / *MÚSICOS Y REPRESENTACIONES*

alto	*alto*	orchestra	*orquesta*
audience	*público*	singer	*cantante*
band	*banda*	song	*canción*
bass	*bajo*	soprano	*soprano*
chorus, choir	*coro*	space	*espacio*
composer	*compositor*	staccato	*staccato*
concert	*concierto*	stage	*escenario*
conductor with baton	*director con batuta*	symphony	*sinfonía*
		tenor	*tenor*
musician	*músico*		
opera	*ópera*		

MUSIC SYMBOLS / *SÍMBOLOS MUSICALES*

symbol	English	Spanish	Italian
>	accent	*acento*	
♪	eighth note	*corchea*	
ⸯ	eighth rest	*silencio de corchea*	
⌒	fermata	*fermata*	
♭	flat	*bemos (bajar el tono)*	
f	loud	*fuerte*	*forte*
ff	very loud	*muy fuerte*	*fortissimo*
♩	half note	*blanca*	
▬	half rest	*silencio de blanca*	
mf	medium loud	*fuerte mediano*	*mezzo forte*
mp	medium soft	*suave mediano*	*mezzo piano*
pp	very soft	*muy suave*	*pianissimo*
p	soft	*suave*	*piano*
♩	quarter note	*negra*	
𝄽	quarter rest	*silencio de negra*	
‖: :‖	repeat	*repetición*	
♯	sharp	*sostenido (elevar medio tono)*	
♬	sixteenth note	*semicorchea*	
ⸯ	sixteenth rest	*silencio de semicorchea*	
☰	staff	*pentagrama*	
𝅝	whole note	*redonda*	
▬	whole rest	*silencio de redonda*	

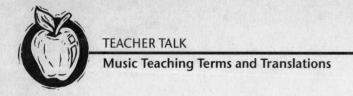

CLASSROOM INSTRUCTIONS / *INSTRUCCIONES*

Instructional Phrases /
Instrucciones

Did the melody go up, go down, or stay the same?	*¿La melodía subió, bajó, o se quedó igual?*
Do what I do.	*Hagan lo que yo hago.*
Don't talk.	*No hablen.*
Echo back.	*Repitan.*
Form a line.	*Formen una línea.*
Go get _____ .	*Trae _____ .*
How does this sound?	*¿Cómo suena esto?*
left hand – right hand	*mano izquierda – mano derecha*
Listen carefully.	*Escuchen atentamente.*
Look at me.	*Mírenme.*
Make this sound.	*Hagan este sonido.*
March in a circle.	*Caminen en círculo.*
partners	*compañeros*
Change partners.	*Cambien de compañero.*
Face your partner.	*Colóquense enfrente de su compañero.*
Select a partner.	*Escojan un compañero.*
Swing your partner.	*Hagan girar a su compañero.*
Pick it up.	*Levántenlo(a).*
Put your hands in your lap.	*Pongan las manos en el regazo.*
Raise your hand.	*Levanten la mano.*
Raise your hand before speaking.	*Levanten la mano cuando quieran hablar.*

ready	*listos*
Ready, begin.	*Listos, empiecen.*
Ready, move.	*Listos, muévanse.*
Ready, play.	*Listos, toquen.*
Ready, sing.	*Listos, canten.*
Stand side by side.	*Párense uno al lado del otro.*
This is called _____ .	*Esto se llama _____ .*
to the left – to the right	*hacia la izquierda – hacia la derecha*
Turn and face me.	*Voltéense y mírenme.*

Instructional Words /
Palabras de Instrucción

begin	*comiencen, empiecen*	return	*devuélvanlo*
bow	*saluden al público*	shout	*griten*
clap	*aplaudan, palmeen*	show me	*enséñame*
conduct	*dirijan*	sing	*canten*
different	*diferente*	slide	*resbalen*
enter	*entren*	speak	*hablen*
jump	*salten*	tiptoe	*anden de puntitas*
listen	*escuchen*	wait	*esperen*
move	*muévanse*	whisper	*susurren*
read	*lean*	write	*escriban*

GREETINGS AND COURTESIES / *SALUDOS Y EXPRESIONES DE CORTESÍA*

Excuse me.	*Con su permiso.*
Good day, everyone.	*Buenos días, niños.*
good try	*bien hecho*
happy birthday	*feliz cumpleaños*
I am the music teacher.	*Yo soy la maestra/el maestro de música.*
please	*por favor*
Thank you.	*Gracias.*
Try again.	*Inténtalo otra vez.*
very good	*muy bien*
You're welcome.	*De nada.*

VI. PRONUNCIATION KEY
A Quick Reference for Spanish

This Key may be used in conjunction with the recordings to help with Spanish pronunciation. Because of regional dialects, Spanish-speaking individuals may pronounce some of these sounds differently.

VOWELS

a	f**a**ther	**u**	m**oo**n
e	ch**a**os	**y**	**y**es (when preceding a vowel;
i	b**ee**		b**ee** (when alone or following a vowel)
o	**o**bey		

CONSONANTS

b **b**ee (at beginning of word, except when word is preceded by *r, s,* or vowels); **b** without touching lips together (between vowels, following *r* or *s*, or when last letter in a syllable)

c **c**at (before *a, o,* or *u*); **s**at (before *e* or *i*); a**cc**ent (when occurs across syllables)

ch **ch**eese

d **d**ay (at beginning of word, except when word is preceded by *r, s,* or vowel); **th**e (between vowels, following *r* or *s,* or when last letter in a syllable)

g **g**o (except before *e* or *i*); Ba**ch** (before *e* or *i*)

gu **g**o (when followed by *e* or *i*—the *u* is silent); **Gw**en (when followed by *a*)

gü **Gw**en

h silent

j strongly aspirated English *h*—**H**o **h**o **h**o!, or mildly aspirated German *ch*—Ba**ch**

ll **y**es (Latin American); mi**lli**on (Castilian)

ñ o**ni**on

q **k**ey (Q always appears with *u*. The *u* is not sounded.)

r bu**tt**er, flipped *r* (when in interior position, final letter of word, or after *s* or *n*); trilled *r* (at beginning of word, except after *s* or *n*)

rr trilled *r* (Ex. Spanish pe**rr**o, ca**rr**o)

s **s**un (usually); **z**ero (before a voiced consonant)

v (See *b,* above.)

x same as Spanish *j* (beginning of word); ki**cks** (within a word)

z **s**un (Latin American) when first or last letter of syllable; **z**ebra (Latin American) before a voiced consonant; **th**ick (Castilian)

Consonants same as English: *f, l, m, n, s, w*
Consonants same as English, except not aspirated: *k, p, t*

Macmillan/McGraw-Hill

Música para todos **for Intermediate Grades**

TEACHER'S NOTES

TEACHER'S NOTES

Indexes

HISPANIC RESOURCES IN *SHARE THE MUSIC*

The following summarizes many of the songs, speech pieces, listenings, literature, and fine art selections from Hispanic/Hispanic American and related cultures in the *Share the Music* series.

Indexes

ALPHABETICAL INDEX OF SONGS

Use this index to locate songs in *Música para todos* and to find additional lesson plans and ideas in the *Share the Music* Teacher's and Pupil Editions.